*Breaking the Chains of Domestic Abuse,
A Comprehensive Guide to Healing and Recovery*

REMOVING THE "D" *from* ANGER

RICKY C. WILLIAMS

Removing The D From Anger Book 2025

Breaking the Chains of Domestic Abuse, a Comprehensive Guide to Healing and Recovery

First published by Life Changing Enterprises LLC 2025

Copyright © 2025 by Ricky C. Williams

All rights reserved. No part of this publication may be reproduced, stored or transmitted in any form or by any means, electronic, mechanical, photocopying, recording, scanning, or otherwise without written permission from the publisher. It is illegal to copy this book, post it to a website, or distribute it by any other means without permission.

Ricky C. Williams asserts the moral right to be identified as the author of this work.

Ricky C. Williams has no responsibility for the persistence or accuracy of URLs for external or third-party Internet Websites referred to in this publication and does not guarantee that any content on such Websites is, or will remain, accurate or appropriate.

First edition

ISBN: 9798991935708

This book was professionally typeset on Reedsy.
Find out more at reedsy.com

For every man who has ever felt misunderstood in his silence, this book is for you. To those fighting silent battles, trying to protect what matters most while struggling to control what rages within, may these pages remind you that you're not broken; you're becoming. And finally, to the boy I once was and the man I chose to become, thank you for not giving up.

"He who conquers others is strong; he who conquers himself is mighty."

—Lao Tzu

Contents

Foreword	vii
Preface	ix
Acknowledgments	xi
Prologue	1
Introduction	3

I -Seneca

II Need Help

1 Dangers of Being in a Toxic Relationships	11
Have You Ever Wondered If This Is Really Love?	11
The Fantasy vs. Reality of Relationships	12
Spotting the Red Flags: Common Signs of Toxic Relationships	13
Emotional and Psychological Fallout	15
Physical Consequences: When Stress Attacks Your Body	16
Social Repercussions: The Silent Isolation	17
Financial Manipulation: When Money Becomes a Weapon	18
The Ghosts That Haunt New Relationships	19
Moving Forward: Your Path to Healing	20

III -Publilius Syrus

2 Damaging Your Partner's Reputation — 25
Have You Ever Realized You Hold Someone's Reputation in Your Hands? — 25
What Reputation Damage Really Means — 26
The Many Ways We Break Trust — 27
How Your Words Shape Someone Else's World — 28
The Personal and Professional Fallout — 28
When the Person You Love Becomes Your Accuser — 29
The Legal Reality: Defamation Is Abuse — 30
Preventing Reputation Damage — 31
Moving Forward with Integrity — 31

IV -Buddha

3 Derogatory Words That Hurt a Person Mentally — 35
Have You Ever Felt Bruised by Words No One Else Could See? — 35
What Verbal Abuse Really Is — 36
The Many Forms Verbal Abuse Can Take — 36
How Words Leave Invisible Scars — 38
How Everyday Language Becomes Abuse — 38
The Cost of Dismissing the Damage — 39
Psychological Mechanisms — 41
Early Wounds That Become Lifelong Patterns — 41
The Role of Substances, Anxiety, and Personality — 42
What This Looks Like in Daily Life — 43
Why Acknowledgment Is the First Step — 43
Preventing Verbal Abuse Before It Starts — 44
The Imperfect Art of Trying — 44

Cleaning Up Your Language	45
Learning a New Way to Speak	45
Moving Forward Without Verbal Abuse	46

V -Edmund Burke

4 Destroying Personal Belongings	49
Destroying Personal Belongings: When Anger Breaks More Than Objects	49
Redefining Abuse: It's Not Just Bruises and Broken Bones	50
The Hidden Logic of Property Destruction	50
The Emotional Fallout: How Broken Things Break Trust	51
Financial Costs: The Price of Rage	52
The Legal Perspective: When Broken Objects Become Criminal Evidence	53
How Property Destruction Becomes a Pattern	55
Why Some People Use Property to Express Power	55
Preventing Destruction: Learning Different Choices	56
Moving Forward Without Breaking More	57

VI -E.W. Howe

5 Devaluing Your Partner's Contribution to the Relationship	61
The Subtle Bruises No One Sees	61
What Devaluation Really Looks Like	62
How It Begins: The Cycle of Idealization and Devaluation	63
Recognizing the Forms of Devaluation	64
Emotional and Psychological Devaluation	64
Physical and Material Devaluation	65
Social and Relational Devaluation	65
Verbal and Nonverbal Devaluation	66

How Devaluation Warps Relationship Dynamics	67
Reclaiming Respect Through Communication	68
Moving From Criticism to Appreciation	68
Moving Forward: Choosing Respect Over Resentment	69

VII — Maya Angelou

6 Disregarding Your Feelings	73
Your Feelings Are Not The Enemy	73
What Emotional Disregard Really Means	74
Examples and Scenarios	75
The Subtle Ways Emotional Disregard Shows Up	76
Why We Dismiss Feelings (Even When We Care)	77
The Impact of Emotional Disregard	78
How to Rebuild Emotional Connection	79
Preventing Emotional Disregard	81
Moving Forward: Your Feelings Matter	82

VIII — Socrates

7 Discontentment Towards Your Partner's Gestures	85
When Everything Seems Fine, But Feels Empty	85
Understanding Discontentment	86
Signs You or Your Partner Are Struggling	87
How Discontentment Impacts the One on the Receiving End	89
Why Appreciation Is Non Negotiable	90
Rebuilding Appreciation and Connection	90
Preventing Discontentment Going Forward	92
Moving Forward: Choosing Appreciation	93

IX —Karen Salmansohn

8 Dysfunctionality Within Your Relationship	97
Dysfunctionality Anyone?	97
Recognizing the Signs of Dysfunction	98
Why Dysfunction Takes Root	99
Common Dysfunctional Dynamics	100
The Impact of Dysfunction	101
Facing Dysfunction with Honesty	103
Steps Toward Change	103
Building a Functional Relationship	104
Moving Forward: No More Dysfunction	105

X - Stephen King

9 Deceiving Your Partner	109
A Slippery Slope No One Sets Out to Climb	109
What Deception Really Means	110
Why People Lie to Those They Love	111
The Impact of Lies on Your Partner	112
How Deception Warps Relationship Dynamics	114
Rebuilding Trust, One Honest Act at a Time	115
Moving Forward, With Courage and Compassion	116

XI - Elisabeth Kubler-Ross

10 Degradation of the Person You Love	119
When the Jokes Stop Feeling Funny	119
Introduction to Degradation	120
Forms of Degradation	120
The Impact on the Victim	121

Why We Degrade the People We Love	124
Addressing Degradation	124
Rebuilding Respect	125
Moving Forward, Together or Apart	126

XII -Eleanor Roosevelt

11 Depreciation of Your Partner's Self-Esteem	129
I Am Too Big to Be Belittled, I Think?	129
Introduction to Self Esteem Depreciation	130
Impact on the Victim	131
Preventing Self Esteem Depreciation	133
Supporting and Rebuilding Self Esteem	134
Moving Forward Together	135

XIII -T.S. Elliot

12 Conclusion	139
Epilogue	142
Afterword	143
References	145
About the Author	152

Foreword

"There comes a moment in every person's life when they have to face the truth, not just about the world around them, but about the world within them. For many men, that truth is uncomfortable, raw, and often buried beneath years of silence, ego, and pain. It shows up in broken relationships, lost opportunities, and regrets that echo long after the outburst fades.

Removing The "D" From Anger is more than a book, it's a mirror, a road map, and a call to action.

Ricky C. Williams has taken one of the most volatile emotions and done something extraordinary with it: he's humanized it, dissected it, and redefined it as a path to emotional mastery. What makes this book so impactful is that Ricky doesn't speak from a pedestal, he speaks from experience. As an anger management coach, certified mediator, and someone who's walked through his own fire, he understands the storm that lives inside so many men. He also understands the courage it takes to confront it.

This book is not about suppressing your anger. It's about reclaiming it, shaping it into something productive, something healing. It teaches you how to turn destruction into discipline, rage into reason, and fury into focus. Ricky blends coaching, real world stories, and practical tools that men can actually use, whether you're a father trying to break generational cycles, a husband fighting to save your relationship, or a professional looking to lead without blowing up under pressure.

I've seen firsthand the transformation that happens when a man decides to stop letting anger speak for him and starts learning how to speak through it. This book will help you do exactly that.

If you're holding this book in your hands, it means you're ready. You're ready to face yourself. You're ready to choose growth over guilt. You're ready to remove the "D", the destruction, from your anger. And that makes you not weak, but strong. Not broken, but rebuilding. Not dangerous, but destined. Welcome to your journey of emotional mastery.

Let this book be your first step and your firmest foundation."

—Rico Gary, Civil Survey PM and Lead Computer Aided Designer

Preface

Anger is one of the most misunderstood emotions in the human experience. For many of us, especially men, anger can feel like the only language we're allowed to speak when we're hurt, overwhelmed, or feel like we're losing control. It becomes a mask we wear, a defense mechanism, a shield. But left unchecked, it can also become a weapon, one that wounds the people we love and sabotages the lives we've worked so hard to build.

I wrote Removing The "D" From Anger not because I mastered anger, but because I had to face mine.

This book is the product of my personal journey and professional experience helping others confront their own emotional struggles. As an anger management coach and certified mediator, I've sat across from men who were desperate to change but didn't know how. I've seen professionals, fathers, partners, and leaders all brought to their knees by the consequences of unresolved anger. But I've also witnessed something more powerful than rage: redemption.

The title, Removing The "D" From Anger, is both a wordplay and a wake-up call. The "D" represents destruction, the damage anger causes when it goes unmanaged. My mission is to help you remove that destruction and transform anger into a force for growth, clarity, and connection. When you take the "D" out of anger, what's left is power. Power to express without hurting. Power to stand up without tearing down. Power to heal.

This book is for men who are ready to take responsibility, not just for their actions, but for their healing. It's also for the people who love them: partners, families, and colleagues who often suffer in silence, hoping for change.

Inside these pages, you won't find lectures or judgment. You'll find tools, stories, and strategies grounded in emotional intelligence, accountability, and compassion. You'll learn how to recognize your triggers, communicate effectively, and regain control in moments where it feels like everything is slipping away.

Anger doesn't make you weak. But refusing to grow through it does.

Let this book be your turning point.

Let this be where the cycle ends and a new chapter begins.

— *Ricky C. Williams*

Anger Management Coach | Mediator | Corporate Trainer

Acknowledgments

As I look back on my life, I see the faces of so many extraordinary people. I'd like to express my deepest gratitude to those who have made an important impact on my life outside of my father, Ivory Williams, and mother, Audrey Williams.

First, to all of my family and extended family, I love you. To my late wife, Makia Williams, I thank you to the moon and back for blessing me with Sydney and Ricky II. You can rest easy knowing that I will fulfill the promise I made to you about raising responsible adults and keeping your memory in their hearts.

To my forever friend and brother David Edmonds, I'm forever grateful to you and Jen for all of the conversations you had with me over the tumultuous moments after Makia's passing. If I had a thousand tongues, I could not thank you enough for what you have done in and for my life. I graciously say Thank you.

To my college roommate, Fraternity Brother, and all-around great friend Jerry Farmer… Thank you. I could not have asked for a more brilliant, strategic, and encouraging friend in the most trivial time in my life. I say Thank you.

To Joe James, thanks for going on this journey with me, brother. Thank you for the heartfelt and meaningful conversations that have impacted my spirit. I love every moment that we have spoken. Thank you for being an amazing man.

To Aaron Vallot, thank you for checking in on me and giving me a space for laughter. You are the only person I know that can bring together so many people with your warmth, kindness, and loving nature. I admire you for who you are and thank you for making our moments together memorable.

To Mike Turner, Jamie Williamson, Daniel McGowen and the Men of One Community Church in Plano, TX. Thank you. I have never met a group of men that prayed so hard for me. There are so many men and women to thank from Ellery, Ray, Tim, Tom, Keith, Talus, Ms. Linda, and the list goes on and on. I say thank you. Your prayers sustained me when I did not know how to pray for myself. I count my blessings every day for having prayer warriors like you.

To Nick Jiles, what else can I say but thank you? To know Nick is to know what true valor and honor are comprised of. Every time I think about how you put your wife and child on a plane to start a new life states away, just so you could drive hours to check on me, it touches my heart. That kind of selflessness says everything about the person you are. I strive daily to have that type of character you innately have. Brother, Thank You.

To my line brothers and my big brothers of Phi Beta Sigma Fraternity Inc. that saw greatness in me, Scotty Johnson, Randolph Butler, Andy Brown, Manny Styles (RIP), Marcus Boyd, Rico Gary, Marcus Tyson, and (D.P.) Cleveland Williams, Thank You. To Torey Page, and all the Grad Chapter members of Iota Mu Sigma, thank you.

To Duchess Britton, who has been like a sister to me and aunt to my kids, thank you. To LaShondra Powell, a woman that has stepped up and become a surrogate mother to my kids and treated them like her own, I say thank you.

To Racquel Ceasar, Nekketta Archie, Lekeisha Shehee, and the ladies of Delta Sigma Theta Sorority, Delta Iota chapter of Grambling State University, thank you for checking on me and the kids. Sydney will follow in her mother's footsteps to continue the amazing legacy of this great organization. Promise!

To my cousins Tank and Jessica, words cannot express how much I love you guys. I can write an entire book on how you loved on us. Your love is the reminder of why family is so important. Thank you from the bottom of my heart.

To all of you that have been mentioned, and the countless others that have impacted me, thank you. Thank you for your love and being wonderful human beings. To have encountered all of you and consider you friends is such a gift. Because of you, I am inspired to live my life to the fullest.

My deepest respect and admiration go to all of you for sharing your precious moments with me. These moments will live in my heart forever. I am eternally grateful.

Finally, I thank God. To God's grace and mercy, which guided me to write this book and to create such phenomenal beings to teach me so many things, too many to mention... Thank you. Thank you for the unknown people that you have set forth to help me complete your purpose on this earth; thank you in advance. I will continue to be on my purpose each and every day to be a blessing to those I have the privilege to serve.

Prologue

Removing The "D" From Anger
By Ricky C. Williams

There was a time in my life when anger controlled everything: my words, my relationships, and my peace of mind. I didn't wake up one day and decide to be angry; it just became the default. It showed up in my tone, in my silence, and in the way I distanced myself from people who cared. And the worst part? I thought it made me strong.

But anger, when left unchecked, doesn't make you powerful. It makes you reactive. It burns bridges you didn't even know you needed. It leaves a trail of regret that apologies can't always fix. For years, I wore it like armor, until I realized it was also a cage.

This book was born from that realization. From my own journey and from the hundreds of stories I've heard from men just like me. The fathers, sons, partners, and leaders, struggling to control a force that always seems one step ahead. Men who were never taught how to express pain without aggression, fear without defensiveness, or sadness without shame.

Removing The "D" From Anger isn't about getting rid of your anger. It's about understanding it. It's about removing the destruction and learning how to use your anger as a tool, not a weapon. Because when you master your emotions, you regain control, not just of your reactions, but of your future.

This book is a conversation I wish someone had had with me years ago. It's not filled with fluff or judgment. It's filled with tools, truths, and transformation. If you're holding this book, chances are you're ready, ready to stop letting anger lead, and ready to lead your anger with intention. This is where that journey begins. Welcome.

Introduction

This short, wisdom rich, and crisply written book couldn't come at a better time. In a world filled with disconnection, disappointment, and digital distractions, real relationships, personal or professional, are suffering. Sadly, much of the conversation around relationships today is drenched in pessimism. Social media is flooded with highlight reels that often mask dysfunction, while studies increasingly show declining satisfaction and rising distrust between partners.

We've reached a point where many people genuinely wonder whether it's even worth it to try anymore. They begin to see relationships as exhausting, unreliable, and, perhaps most dangerously, a waste of time and effort.

But avoiding love, connection, or accountability because of fear or frustration is a costly long-term mistake. And that's exactly what this book is here to address.

In Removing The D from Anger, I, Ricky C. Williams, invite you to take a real, honest look at how anger affects your relationships, not just as an emotion, but as a pattern of choices, responses, and learned behaviors. My goal is not to lecture you about being calm or patient but to help you understand your anger, where it comes from, and how to stop it from turning into something destructive.

Because here's the truth: **no relationship is always peaceful**. Conflict is normal. Disagreements are inevitable. But dysfunction doesn't have to be.

As an anger management coach, I've helped countless people navigate the difficult, emotional process of unpacking their pain, recognizing their triggers, and building healthier habits. I've seen what happens when people sit on the sidelines, refusing to invest in their own emotional growth: relationships wither, potential is lost, and cycles repeat. But I've also seen what's possible when people lean in, do the work, and take full ownership of their emotional world.

This book is about learning how to press that reset button, not just when things fall apart, but before they do. It's about developing constructive responses to anger, rather than destructive ones. And most importantly, it's about valuing the people you love, instead of devaluing them through silence, blame, or impulsive reactions.

You'll learn:

1. How destructive anger patterns form in relationships
2. The legal and emotional consequences of those patterns
3. How to shift from reaction to regulation
4. How to communicate in ways that restore, not rupture
5. And how to stop hurting the people you want to hold onto

Anger is not inherently wrong. It's human. What matters is how you use it. Do you use it to defend your ego? Or to demand deeper understanding? Do you shut down? Or step up with clarity?

By exploring the early beliefs, traumas, and emotional histories that shape your anger, this book will help you better understand yourself and, ultimately, help you connect more meaningfully with others.

If you're ready to go further, I encourage you to join on my website, **Removing The D from Anger Course**. It's designed for those who want practical, real-life tools to better manage their emotions, communicate clearly, and build stronger, more respectful relationships, both personally and professionally.

INTRODUCTION

You don't need to be perfect to build something beautiful. But you do need to be intentional. Let's start there, together.

I

-Seneca

"Every new beginning comes from some other beginning's end."

II

Need Help

To those people who will never settle for less than an amazing relationship both personal and professional, do share, and for immediate help from me go to:
psychologytoday.com/profile/125849
–Ricky C. Williams

1

Dangers of Being in a Toxic Relationships

Have You Ever Wondered If This Is Really Love?

Let's be honest for a moment. Have you ever found yourself staring at your phone, replaying a fight over and over, wondering, *"Is this really good for me?"* Maybe you sit alone quiet after another argument, the room dark except for the glow of your screen, and ask yourself, *"How did I end up here? How did things get so complicated, so painful?"* If you have, you're far from alone. **I've sat with countless people who quietly whisper these same questions in the stillness of their lives, unsure if what they're experiencing is love, or something far more damaging.**

The line between an ordinary disagreement and a harmful, toxic pattern isn't always clear or easy to see. Often, it sneaks up on you. One day, you're brushing off harsh words as *"just stress"* or *"a bad mood."* The next, you're losing sleep, doubting your worth, and feeling smaller, like your very essence is shrinking under the weight of constant criticism or cold indifference.

What's especially sobering is that this isn't just about romantic relationships. Sometimes, it's a parent's relentless criticism that leaves invisible scars you carry into adulthood. Sometimes, it's a sibling whose unpredictable temper makes your heart race every time the phone rings. It could be a partner, a friend, or even a boss. No matter the source, the effect is the same: a slow, insidious erosion of your peace, your confidence, and your sense of self.

Arguments that escalate into shouting matches, icy silences that stretch on for days, and those subtle, cutting remarks that chip away at your confidence, these are not just "normal" relationship struggles. They are warning signs. And you should pay attention to them. Because toxic relationships can hijack your peace of mind, your health, and your very identity faster than you might imagine.

Here's the truth:

Toxic relationships are alarmingly common. They lurk in the shadows of friendships, family ties, and partnerships alike. Learning to recognize them isn't just smart, it's essential for your survival. This chapter is your first step toward understanding what toxicity looks like, how it seeps into your life, and why you deserve so much more than this.

The Fantasy vs. Reality of Relationships

Picture this:

You're in a relationship where you feel safe, cherished, and completely at ease. You know, deep down, that no matter what happens, you're secure. You trust your partner. You feel free to be your whole, authentic self, flaws, quirks, and all.

I think, deep down, most of us hold a vision of what love or connection is supposed to feel like. You picture something safe and warm, the place you can finally exhale. A relationship where you don't have to tiptoe or hide the parts of yourself that feel too tender.

Most of us hold onto this vision, even if our reality looks very different.

We crave that calm, abundant love story, the kind that feels like a gentle embrace rather than a tightrope walk over broken glass.

But if your relationship feels more like walking on eggshells, constantly drained of joy and shrinking to fit someone else's expectations, it's time to call it what it is: **toxic.**

You find yourself measuring your words, apologizing for things you didn't do, and explaining to yourself why you should stay. If you've ever convinced yourself it would get better, "if you just tried harder," you're not alone. I've heard those same words from people of every age, background, and education level.

Toxic relationships are built on a cocktail of emotional stress, mind games, and slow, creeping damage to your self-worth. And the longer you stay, the more your mind and body absorb that poison.

Here's the simplest way I can say this:

A relationship that asks you to shrink will never help you grow, and recognizing these signs can literally save your life, and your sanity.

Spotting the Red Flags: Common Signs of Toxic Relationships

Toxic dynamics don't always look like screaming matches or broken dishes. More often, they're quiet patterns that wear you down until you can't remember what calm feels like.

You might notice you're always on edge, waiting for the next accusation. You might feel your energy drain every time you see their name pop up on your screen. Over time, these moments collect like pebbles in your pockets, making everything feel heavier.

Sometimes, it's a sudden eruption, an explosive argument that leaves you shaken. Other times, it's the cold, dismissive silence that makes you question your own sanity. I've seen people endure years of this slow unraveling because they were taught that love means endurance. But love isn't meant to feel like punishment.

Here's where things get specific. If you see yourself in any of these, you're not imagining it:

- **You constantly feel unsupported or unsafe.** It's like being on stage without knowing your lines, dreading the next jab or criticism.
- **They go on explosive rants.** You walk on eggshells, never sure what will set them off.
- **They withhold affection to control you.** Silence becomes a weapon, and you feel starved for reassurance.
- **You're always unhappy or stressed.** Even on the "good days," you can't shake the tension.
- **Passive aggressive communication is the norm.** Think: sarcasm, guilt trips, stonewalling.
- **They scrutinize everything you do.** You're judged, corrected, and second guessed, constantly.
- **They lie, cheat, or gaslight you.** You start questioning your own memory.
- **They shame you into feeling small.** It's always your fault, never theirs.
- **They erase your identity.** You become an extension of their ego.
- **They're possessive.** Every friendship, every hobby, scrutinized or resented.
- **Pessimism clouds every conversation.** Nothing you do is ever good enough.

Here's the kicker:
Once you're in this cycle, honesty is often the first casualty. They deny, deflect, and accuse. The silence between you grows heavy, and your spirit starts to dim, but your hope for change keeps you tethered.

Emotional and Psychological Fallout

I've sat across from so many clients whose eyes told me everything before they said a word. The fear. The self-doubt. The quiet desperation of someone who's been diminished one insult at a time. I wish I could tell you these patterns were harmless. But I've watched them strip the joy out of bright, resilient people.

When you're constantly belittled or manipulated, your body responds as if it's under attack. You might find yourself flinching at sudden noises or losing focus at work because you're replaying conversations in your mind, wondering what you could have said differently.

Over time, the anxiety settles into your bones. It becomes a constant companion, whispering that you aren't good enough or strong enough to leave. I've sat across from clients whose eyes held the same tired ache, whose voices fell into a hush as they described the moment they stopped recognizing themselves.

Research has shown that people who spend years in these environments face higher rates of depression, anxiety, and post-traumatic stress. The data is clear, but the lived experience feels even more overwhelming. When you're in it, you start to believe this is just your life now.

I've watched people lose everything, homes, careers, even the respect of their own families, because of a toxic relationship.

Here are just a few ways the damage shows up emotionally:

- Crushing hopelessness
- Depression that won't budge
- Total lack of motivation
- Anxiety that wraps around your ribs
- Emotional reactivity that leaves you exhausted

And research backs this up:

- **2024 APA/NIMH studies:** Those with a history of toxic relationships were significantly more likely to experience depression.
- **Domestic abuse survivors:** At high risk of PTSD.
- **Young people exposed to four or more adverse events:** Seventeen times more likely to attempt suicide.

The scariest part?

The person who causes this damage often acts like they're blameless, like you're the problem. And that gaslighting can make you feel insane.

Physical Consequences: When Stress Attacks Your Body

You've probably heard it before: "It's not just in your head." And it's true. One of the cruelest things about toxic relationships is how they don't only hurt your spirit, they hurt your health.

The stress of feeling unsafe, unloved, or unseen triggers a cascade of chemical responses in your body. You may notice you're getting sick more often, sleeping poorly, or feeling exhausted no matter how much you rest.

Chronic stress elevates cortisol levels, which can wreak havoc on your immune system, digestion, memory, and even the way you process emotions. I've worked with people who developed chronic pain, migraines, and unexplained illnesses that only began to heal once they left the relationship.

If any of this feels familiar, if your body feels like it's carrying too much, please know that it's not your imagination. This is what happens when love turns into survival. Over time, this biochemical onslaught can age you, weaken your immunity, and break your spirit.

Here's what prolonged toxicity can look like physically:

- Getting sick all the time
- Struggling with insomnia
- Digestive problems (that mysterious stomach pain? Yep)
- Constant fatigue
- Random body aches
- Unexplained weight changes
- Inflammation that lingers

I say this to every client:
You can't think clearly when you're in survival mode. When you're exhausted, overwhelmed, and scared, you can't thrive.

But here's the good news, this doesn't have to be your forever. You can learn to break free.

Social Repercussions: The Silent Isolation

Another hidden cost of a toxic relationship is the quiet, creeping loneliness that follows.

You may begin to drift away from friends and family, either because you're too tired to pretend everything's fine or because you're ashamed to admit how bad it's gotten. Sometimes, the person you're with demands your loyalty in ways that force you to choose between them and everyone else. And sometimes, the people who love you step back because they don't know how to help.

It can feel as if you've lost your place in the world. If you've ever sat alone and wondered why nobody calls anymore, if you've felt the sting of your own isolation, please hear this: it isn't your fault. **Toxic people know how to make you feel like you're the problem, so you don't question their behavior.**

Let's be honest:

This isolation is exactly what toxic people want. It makes you easier to control. Take a moment. Grab a pen or highlighter. Which of these describes your life right now?

- You've lost touch with people you love.
- Your work and finances are slipping.
- Your kids are withdrawing or acting out because the home feels unsafe.
- Friends avoid visiting because of your partner's behavior.
- You feel completely alone.
- You're emotionally, financially, and mentally drained.

If you nodded to any of these, you're not alone, and you deserve support.

Financial Manipulation: When Money Becomes a Weapon

Toxic relationships love to twist trust into control, and money is an easy lever.

I've noticed that financial manipulation often hides in plain sight. It doesn't always look like outright theft. Sometimes, it's a slow encroachment on your autonomy, a partner who insists you merge accounts "to build trust," or a family member who racks up debt in your name.

It starts with small requests, maybe a guilt trip about helping them out "just this once." But over time, the imbalance grows until you feel trapped by obligations you never agreed to.

Money is one of the simplest ways to keep someone dependent. When you can't access your own resources, it becomes much harder to leave.

And if you've been told that protecting your finances is selfish, I'd like you to consider that it might be one of the most self-respecting decisions you ever make.

Here's how you'll recognize it:

- They tie themselves to your finances, "for your own good."
- Money talks are taboo. You're expected to tolerate overspending and secrecy.
- They claim ownership of everything because you're "a team."
- They limit your access to your own funds.
- They demand a running tally of every purchase.

I know it's hard to say, "no" to people you love. But boundaries are non-negotiable. Protecting your financial freedom is protecting your survival.

The Ghosts That Haunt New Relationships

Even after you walk away, the impact lingers. You may step into a new relationship carrying invisible baggage, a suspicion of kindness, a reflex to expect betrayal, a fear that any happiness is temporary. You might find yourself bracing for criticism that never comes, or doubting your own instincts even when everything is fine.

This is what happens when your trust has been broken too many times. Your nervous system tries to protect you by scanning for threats that aren't there anymore.

You're not broken, nor is it weakness. You're protecting yourself the only way you know how, which is evidence of how strong you had to be to survive.

Here's how these past wounds show up:

- Trust issues and paranoia
- Reluctance to be vulnerable
- Constant self-doubt
- The belief that you're destined to be hurt again

This is why understanding the roots of your pain matters. It's not about blaming yourself, it's about reclaiming your power.

Moving Forward: Your Path to Healing

If you've recognized yourself in any of these words, take a breath. Let's be clear: **Toxic relationships aren't the end of your story.** Nothing about this makes you weak or unworthy. If anything, the fact that you're still here, still searching for answers, means you haven't given up on yourself.

Healing from a toxic relationship is not a single decision. It's a series of small, brave choices to believe that you deserve better. It's learning to trust your own voice again. It's giving yourself permission to hope. Think of them as a hard-earned education in what you'll never settle for again. The pain you've endured, it's proof that you're stronger than you think.

This chapter is a beginning, not a verdict. You don't have to force yourself to heal overnight. You don't have to rush this. You don't have to do it alone. But you do deserve to know that peace and love are possible. You do deserve time, grace, and support. The lessons you've learned will become your guide as you rebuild, reclaiming your worth, and start designing a life where you feel safe, fulfilled, and free.

In the next chapter, I'll walk with you. We'll unpack how your partner can **Damage Your Reputation.**

III

-Publilius Syrus

"A good reputation is more valuable than money."

2

Damaging Your Partner's Reputation

Have You Ever Realized You Hold Someone's Reputation in Your Hands?

It's strange how easily we forget that the things we say about someone have a life of their own. You might think of words as disposable, just little flickers of feeling in the heat of a moment. You vent to a friend, share a private frustration, or exaggerate a detail to make your story more compelling. You tell yourself it doesn't matter.

But then, a week or a month later, you hear your own words coming back to you, echoing in someone else's voice, reshaped into something colder and more permanent.

When you're in a relationship, especially an intimate one, you're entrusted with an invisible power: you have access to someone's private world. Their struggles, insecurities, and unguarded moments. And with that trust comes a responsibility to protect the story they can't always tell for themselves.

When you break that trust, you're not just having a harmless rant. You're altering how the world sees them and, often, how they see themselves.

This chapter is about that invisible line. The one between honesty and harm. Between accountability and vengeance. It's about how the simple act of telling a story, especially when you're hurt, can quietly devastate another person's life.

What Reputation Damage Really Means

We usually hear the word "defamation" and think of tabloids or celebrities. But you don't have to be famous to suffer when your reputation is attacked.

At its core, **reputation damage** happens any time your words or actions cause others to see someone in a harsher, uglier light, especially if what you're sharing isn't fair or true.

Picture this. You and your partner have a fight, one of those nights when everything feels too raw to handle alone. You call a friend. Your voice shakes. Maybe you say something like, "They're always screaming at me," or "They're completely unstable." In that moment, you feel justified. You're hurt, you want comfort, and you're not thinking about the aftermath.

But your friend, who once thought well of your partner, can't unhear those words. The image you planted will stick. Maybe they'll tell someone else. Maybe they'll start to look at your partner differently.

Over time, this becomes a web of misunderstanding. And if you're not careful, your version of the story will become the only one that matters.

The Many Ways We Break Trust

Reputation damage doesn't always look obvious. It doesn't always involve shouting or making dramatic accusations. Sometimes, it's a much quieter, subtle nudge, a half-truth, or a knowing smirk that leaves someone else to fill in the blanks.

In my work, I've seen all kinds of patterns. Some are deliberate, born from spite. Others are impulsive, rooted in pain or fear. But the impact is often the same.

Here are a few ways it shows up:

- **Slander.** Telling lies about your partner's character or actions, especially to people who trust you as a source.
- **Gossip.** Sharing private details, not to get help or clarity, but to entertain or recruit sympathy.
- **Exposing private content.** Posting photos, screenshots, or recordings your partner never agreed to share.
- **Libel.** Publishing accusations, whether it's a Facebook rant or a blog post, without evidence.
- **Breaking confidentiality.** Revealing secrets your partner trusted you to keep.
- **Public shaming.** Gathering allies to confront or humiliate your partner.

You might justify these behaviors in the moment. You might think, *"They deserve it,"* or *"I need people to know what I'm dealing with."*

But here's the hard truth: no matter how righteous your anger feels, those actions cross a line that's difficult to uncross.

How Your Words Shape Someone Else's World

One of the most painful consequences of reputation damage is how far it can reach.

Because you're close to your partner, your opinions carry more weight than anyone else's. People assume you have special insight. They take your words seriously, even when they shouldn't.

I've seen this play out in countless ways:

- A manager hears you complain that your partner is "lazy" or "unreliable." Suddenly, promotions disappear. Projects get reassigned.
- A parent reconsiders passing down property because you've painted your partner as irresponsible.
- A circle of friends stops inviting your partner to gatherings because they've heard you say, "They always ruin everything."

These shifts don't usually happen all at once. They unfold in tiny increments: an email that never arrives, a conversation that trails off, a look that lingers too long.

And soon, your partner is standing in the wreckage, wondering how they became the villain in a story they didn't even know was being told.

The Personal and Professional Fallout

When you damage someone's reputation, you don't just impact how others see them. You also change how they see themselves.

I've sat across from people whose entire sense of self had been eroded by a steady stream of whispered doubts and public callouts. They stopped trusting their instincts. They started to believe they really were broken, unreliable, and unlovable.

In practical terms, reputation damage can affect:

- **Employment.** Studies show that 47% of hiring managers factor social media and online gossip into their decisions. One rumor can mean a lost job offer or an awkward dismissal.
- **Legal credibility.** If your partner ends up in court, whether for custody, contracts, or other disputes, your words can be used against them.
- **Mental health.** The loneliness and shame of being misrepresented often lead to anxiety, depression, and withdrawal.
- **Support networks.** Friends and family may distance themselves, unsure of who to believe.

It's not uncommon for victims to feel they've lost everything—security, connection, and purpose because of a few sentences shared without care.

When the Person You Love Becomes Your Accuser

If you've ever been on the receiving end of this, you know how gutting it feels.

There is a particular grief in realizing that someone you trusted has become the architect of your humiliation. Your sense of safety evaporates. Every social interaction feels like a trap, every text a potential exposure.

You might start to wonder:

- What else have they said about me?
- Is there anyone who still believes in me?
- How do I fix what I can't see?

Over time, this vigilance calcifies into self-protection. You stop sharing. You stop showing up. You stop hoping for understanding.

The Legal Reality: Defamation Is Abuse

Some people think of defamation as a civil issue, something that only matters if you're wealthy enough to sue. But in reality, it's a recognized form of harm.

If your words are proven false and damaging, you can be held accountable through:

- **Slander.** Spoken statements that harm someone's reputation.
- **Libel.** Written or published statements that cause harm.

Libel is usually treated more seriously because it leaves a paper trail. Screenshots, emails, and posts become evidence that can't be dismissed as hearsay.

Victims can sue for:

- Loss of income
- Emotional distress
- Damaged relationships
- Reputational harm

If this sounds intimidating, that's because it is. And it should be. Because the power to shape someone's life with your words is not something to take lightly.

Preventing Reputation Damage

If you're reading this and feeling a knot in your stomach, take a breath. This is not an indictment of your character. It's an invitation to pause and reflect.

Maybe you've spoken out of anger. Maybe you've shared too much with too many people. Maybe you've felt so hurt that you believed retaliation was the only way to feel seen. But, you have another choice.

Here are a few ways to begin:

- **Pause before you share.** If you wouldn't say it to your partner's face, think twice before saying it to anyone else.
- **Seek help instead of gossip.** A therapist or coach can help you process your feelings safely.
- **Apologize if you've crossed a line.** Owning your part is the first step to rebuilding trust.
- **Commit to privacy.** Some things are meant to stay between you and the person you love.
- **Give space.** If your partner is hurt, respect their boundaries as they decide whether and how to forgive.

Moving Forward with Integrity

Here's what I know for sure: **You are not defined by your worst moment.**

If you've damaged someone's reputation, it doesn't mean you're beyond redemption. It means you have an opportunity, a chance to learn how to hold your words more gently.

And if you're the one whose name has been tarnished, please know that your worth is not up for debate. You are still whole, still worthy of love, still entitled to dignity. You deserve relationships that honor your truth and protect your story. **And you deserve the chance to start again.**

In the chapter ahead, we'll look at other forms of hidden harm, like **Derogatory Words That Hurt a Person Mentally.**

IV

-Buddha

"Better than a thousand hollow words is one word that brings peace."

3

Derogatory Words That Hurt a Person Mentally

Have You Ever Felt Bruised by Words No One Else Could See?

It's funny how people will look for bruises on your arms, cuts on your face, or casts on your limbs to measure whether you've been harmed. If they can't see evidence, if there's no scar or police report, it's easy for them to assume it wasn't "real."

But here's the truth: some of the deepest wounds never show. They live in the space between your ears, replaying every time you close your eyes.

You might remember exactly what was said, word for word, years later. Maybe you still hear that voice in your head: the one that told you that you were worthless, unlovable, or stupid. Maybe you've spent countless hours trying to scrub those phrases out of your memory, only to find they've left an imprint you can't quite erase.

This is the invisible power of verbal abuse. It doesn't leave a mark on your skin, but it can permanently damage your sense of self.

And that is just as real, and just as devastating, as any other form of violence.

What Verbal Abuse Really Is

Some people tell themselves that as long as they're not throwing punches, they're not doing anything wrong. That if their partner isn't crying or flinching, the damage can't be that serious.

But abuse isn't only about what your hands do. It's about what your words do.

Verbal abuse is when language is used, sometimes subtly, sometimes explosively, to create fear, exert control, or chip away at someone's confidence (Gordon, n.d.).

Imagine hearing nothing but criticism day after day. Imagine waking up every morning wondering if today will be the day you'll finally be "good enough," only to be reminded, again, that you'll never measure up.

Even if there is no yelling or name calling, the effect is cumulative. Over time, you stop trusting your own thoughts. You question your worth. You wonder if you deserve anything better.

And that's exactly what makes verbal abuse so insidious. It can be hidden behind excuses: "I was just being honest," or "You're too sensitive." But it isn't honesty, if it's meant to wound. It isn't sensitivity, if it's a reaction to repeated humiliation. *It's ABUSE!*

The Many Forms Verbal Abuse Can Take

Sometimes, people imagine verbal abuse as screaming insults or hurling profanity. But it doesn't always look that obvious. Often, it's woven into everyday interactions so skillfully that you don't recognize it until the damage is done.

I've seen people in my coaching practice who didn't realize they were being verbally abused until years had passed. By then, their confidence was depleted, their energy spent trying to keep the peace.

Here are some common ways it shows up:

- **Nitpicking everything.** Maybe you feel like you can't do anything right, your cooking, your laugh, the way you walk. These criticisms aren't about improvement. They're about control.
- **Chronic denial.** If every disagreement ends with your experience being invalidated, "That's not what happened," "You're imagining things," you learn not to trust yourself. Over time, this becomes gaslighting.
- **Harsh criticism.** It's one thing to give constructive feedback. It's another to tear someone down so they feel small, stupid, or ashamed.
- **Gaslighting.** This is the art of making you doubt your own reality, telling you that you're "crazy" or "too emotional," even when your feelings are valid.
- **Controlling conversations.** Some people steer every discussion, deciding what topics are allowed and which ones are off limits. Over time, you forget what it feels like to have an equal voice.
- **Playing the perpetual victim.** This tactic flips accountability/responsibility on its head. No matter what happens, it's always your fault. You're always the one who "made them" act that way.
- **Explosive outbursts.** Shouting, slamming doors, or sudden rage is used to intimidate and silence you.
- **Subtle threats or taunts.** Not every threat is loud. Sometimes, it's a quiet comment that leaves you wondering if you're safe or if you'll ever be respected again (Gordon, n.d.).

What makes these tactics so effective is their unpredictability. You never know which version of your partner you'll get. So, you learn to tiptoe, to self edit, to avoid anything that might trigger another attack.

How Words Leave Invisible Scars

You might wonder why certain words feel so damaging. After all, can a single comment really change how you see yourself?
The answer is yes.
When you hear something often enough, it starts to embed itself in your identity. You start to see yourself through the lens of the person who keeps telling you that you're less than.

Imagine carrying around a mental tape that plays on repeat:

- *"You're worthless."*
- *"You're unlovable."*
- *"You can't do anything right."*

Eventually, you internalize those words, and they become part of your narrative. Even if you leave the relationship, the echoes can stay with you for years.

This is why many survivors of verbal abuse struggle with depression, anxiety, and PTSD, conditions that are often harder to treat because the damage is invisible, but constant.

How Everyday Language Becomes Abuse

Verbal abuse doesn't have to be loud or explicit. Sometimes, it's hidden in small phrases, the ones we convince ourselves are harmless.

Consider these examples:

- *"You're overreacting."* Translation: Your feelings don't matter.
- *"No one else would ever love you."* Translation: You're lucky to have me, so stop complaining.
- *"I was just joking."* Translation: Your pain is funny to me.
- *"You're too sensitive."* Translation: It's your fault you feel hurt.
- *"Why can't you be more like [someone else]?"* Translation: You'll never be good enough.

Each time you hear these messages, you shrink a little more. You start to believe that maybe you really are too sensitive, too needy, too flawed.

The Cost of Dismissing the Damage

It's easy to dismiss verbal abuse as "not that serious." But consider this: when your sense of self has been chipped away over time, it's no less real than a broken bone.

Research has shown that people who endure chronic verbal abuse experience:

- Severe anxiety and panic attacks.
- Long term depression and hopelessness.
- Difficulty trusting others, even those who are safe.
- A diminished sense of self worth.

When you downplay your own pain, or when others do, you're robbed of the chance to heal.

Examples and Scenarios

Scotty lived his entire childhood abused by his stepmother. For as long as he can remember, he was always described as a disgusting person to be around. According to her, he was always doing something wrong. The games he played were always too loud. He didn't score well enough on his exams. She liked to tell him that he would never amount to anything when he grew up. Unsurprisingly, he ended up internalizing these words as he grew up. Even as a college graduate with a good job, Scotty still doubted himself. He fretted about whether he was disgusting when he hung out with his girlfriend, who loved him. Deep down, he never trusted that anyone could love him. He doubted that his girlfriend liked him genuinely. He doubted whether he was the kind of person who deserved a faithful relationship. How could someone love him when he could never give enough effort to be appreciated? He didn't believe that he was worthy of love after a childhood of being told that he would never amount to anything. His stepmother hardly ever touched him, let alone complimented him.

Alex loved his parents and did not doubt that they loved him back. The only issue is that they only accepted the idea of what a successful person appeared to be. They didn't want him to interact with people they didn't know. They wanted him to engage in certain extracurricular activities. They wanted him to only excel in his schoolwork and not socially. His friends considered them strange. For a year, Alex hid his romantic relationship with a long term girlfriend. Despite his efforts, his parents managed to gain intel on him and his whereabouts. On the day that they found Alex to be engaging in sexual conduct with his girlfriend, his parents vowed to cut off his financial support, disallow him from applying to college, and break him apart from his friend group. They even talked his grandparents into cutting off his trust fund. As a consenting adult of 18 years old, Alex feels oppressed and heavily conflicted with the way his parents limit his social life. They only express themselves to their child lovingly, hardly ever raising their voices at him. However, Alex's parents' involvement in his life severely violates his rights, emotionally and financially. Abuse does not have to be physical to be intrusive and traumatizing.

Psychological Mechanisms

There's something almost unthinkable about it, how someone can swear they care for you, then turn around and say things that hollow you out from the inside. Or lash out in ways that leave invisible bruises you spend years trying to heal.

It's easy, when you've been hurt, to tell yourself it's because you were flawed, too sensitive, too needy. It's even easier for the person doing the hurting to convince themselves they had no other choice, that their outburst was your fault, and that you somehow provoked it.

But the truth is, abuse almost never starts because a person wakes up one morning and decides to be cruel. **It grows from much older wounds, unresolved pain, unmet needs, and beliefs about love and power that were learned long before your relationship began.**

That doesn't excuse it. Nothing ever does. But if you're going to free yourself from the cycle, whether you've been the one harmed or the one harming, it helps to understand what fuels it.

Early Wounds That Become Lifelong Patterns

To really understand why someone lashes out, you have to look beneath the surface.

Think back to childhood. **So many of us are shaped by environments that feel chaotic, neglectful, or frightening.** Maybe the person who later becomes abusive was once a child who felt powerless. A child who never knew when the next blow, physical or emotional, would come. A child who learned that love meant compliance, or that anger was the only way to feel seen.

When you grow up without stable love or healthy modeling, your nervous system wires itself around survival. You learn to protect yourself by controlling others. You learn to numb your fear by blaming someone else.

This isn't an excuse for abuse. It's a map of how unresolved pain becomes a weapon.

Hammond (2017) writes about this internal instability, how it breeds deep insecurity and makes self worth feel conditional and brittle. So, when an adult who never learned another way feels threatened, maybe by rejection, conflict, or the idea of not being "enough," they lash out.

In that moment, anger becomes a shortcut to power. It feels like relief, a surge of control that briefly mutes the old fears of inadequacy. But the relief doesn't last. And when it fades, the shame creeps back in, usually so unbearable that it has to be buried again.

And so the cycle repeats.

The Role of Substances, Anxiety, and Personality

Trauma isn't the only factor that contributes to these patterns. Chronic anxiety, depression, substance abuse, and certain personality disorders can also play a role.

Someone who never learned how to self soothe, who feels hijacked by emotion at the first sign of stress, might resort to yelling or intimidation simply because they have no other toolkit.

People who grew up around addiction may also internalize that lashing out is normal. They might drink or use drugs to dull their fear or sadness, only to find their anger erupting uncontrollably.

Over time, these learned behaviors start to feel like "just who I am." And when you add in a culture that often glorifies violence, where movies and social media treat rage as entertainment, it's no wonder so many people never question their own reactions.

But here's the most important truth: None of these factors make someone abusive. They help explain it, but they don't justify it. **Every person has the capacity to pause, reflect, and choose a different**

response.

The problem is, denial keeps them from ever reaching that crossroads. And denial is what leaves victims carrying the burden of someone else's pain.

What This Looks Like in Daily Life

If you've lived with someone who can't own their behavior, you know how exhausting it is to tiptoe around their moods. You probably became an expert in reading micro expressions, sensing when the energy in the room shifted, and bracing for the next storm.

And if you've been the one doing the hurting, you may have told yourself you were justified. That you were only reacting to provocation. But if you look deeper, you may find that the person you were punishing wasn't the true source of your rage.

It was never really about them. It was about the ghosts of your past, the fears you never named, and the shame you never learned how to sit with. The trouble is, until you admit this, nothing changes.

Why Acknowledgment Is the First Step

If you've recognized yourself in these descriptions, as the person who has hurt others or as the one who has been hurt, I want you to know this: you are not alone. And you are not irredeemable.

Admitting that you have a problem is the bravest thing you can do. Because it means you're finally choosing accountability over avoidance.

It doesn't mean you have to drown in shame. Shame will keep you stuck. But responsibility will set you free.

Because only when you see the mechanisms clearly, the denial, the projection, the learned helplessness, can you start to dismantle them.

Preventing Verbal Abuse Before It Starts

Maybe you're thinking, *"But what if I'm too far gone? What if I've done too much damage?"*

You haven't. Nothing will erase the past, but everything you do from this moment forward can be different.

When you feel that surge of frustration, pause. Remember that life already has enough pain without adding yours to someone else's.

Over time, unmanaged anger becomes a slow poison in your relationships. The people who care about you may start to pull away, not because they don't love you, but because they have to protect themselves.

Here's what I want you to know: *"If connection matters to you, if love matters, then you have to choose it over the short term satisfaction of lashing out."*

The Imperfect Art of Trying

No matter how much you learn about communication, there will still be moments when you lose your footing. You'll say something you regret, or you'll shut down or explode.

That doesn't mean you're failing. It means you're human. What matters is that you keep coming back to the work, asking yourself hard questions, apologizing when you need to, and making space for the discomfort that comes with growth.

This process will never be linear. Some days, you'll feel like you've made progress. Other days, you'll wonder if you've changed at all.

But every time you pause instead of reacting, you're building a new pattern. One that honors both your own pain and the humanity of the person in front of you.

Cleaning Up Your Language

You can never fully know what someone else finds hurtful, because everyone carries a different history. But you can choose to be intentional and thoughtful about the words you use.

Here are a few principles to guide you:

- **Be mindful of personal information.** If someone trusted you with a story, it's not yours to use against them later.
- **Avoid discriminatory language.** Racist, or sexist remarks aren't "harmless jokes." They're wounds that can reopen old traumas.
- **Don't assume superiority.** No matter what someone has done, you don't get to decide they are less human.

Language is powerful. It can build bridges or start wars. It can heal or destroy. The choice is always yours (Sterbenz & Davis, 2020).

Learning a New Way to Speak

If you've recognized yourself in these patterns, as the victim or the person who caused harm, it doesn't mean you're doomed. It means you're aware. And awareness is the doorway to change.

Here are steps you can take:

- **Pause before you speak.** If you're angry, step away until you can respond without cruelty.
- **Own your words.** If you've said something hurtful, acknowledge it without excuses.
- **Practice empathy.** Imagine how your words will feel in someone

else's mind days or years from now.
- **Seek help.** If you struggle to break these habits, coaching can help you understand why, and how to stop.
- **Set boundaries.** If you're on the receiving end, you have every right to ask for respect and to leave if you don't get it.

Moving Forward Without Verbal Abuse

Healing from patterns of verbal abuse, whether you were the one harmed or the one causing harm, doesn't happen overnight. But it does happen. It happens every time you choose honesty over denial, accountability over blame, and compassion over pride.

It happens when you learn to sit with uncomfortable emotions instead of weaponizing them. It happens when you decide that your legacy will not be defined by the worst thing you've done or the worst thing that happened to you. **You deserve peace. And so do the people you love.**

In the next chapter, we'll explore the negative effects of **Destroying Personal Belongings,** the emotional and psychological impact, and ways to prevent destruction.

Let's continue

V

-Edmund Burke

"Rage and phrenzy will pull down more in half an hour than prudence, deliberation, and foresight can build up in a hundred years."

4

Destroying Personal Belongings

Destroying Personal Belongings: When Anger Breaks More Than Objects

It's strange how quickly it can happen. One moment, your living room looks exactly the same as it did when you woke up that morning. The next, something you cared about, a photograph, a vase, a book, a favorite shirt, is lying in pieces at your feet.

And maybe what's even stranger is how quiet it can feel. Sure, there was yelling or the crash of whatever hit the wall, but afterward, there's this hush, like the house itself is holding its breath.

In that quiet, you might feel your stomach turn as you realize what's been lost. Sometimes it isn't about the object's price. It's about what it symbolized: safety, stability, the small proof that you have a life and a space that belongs to you.

The first time it happens, you might tell yourself it was a fluke. Just a bad moment. But when property destruction becomes a pattern, when it's used as a threat, a punishment, or a twisted way to show who's in charge, it stops being an outburst. It becomes abuse.

And if you've been the person who's thrown, smashed, or broken things in anger, you probably already know, deep down, that the momentary rush of release isn't worth what it costs afterward.

Redefining Abuse: It's Not Just Bruises and Broken Bones

For a long time, most people believed that domestic abuse was only about visible harm, bruises, cuts, black eyes. Something you could point to in a police report or photograph.

That narrow definition gave countless people permission to excuse other kinds of harm: the insults, the threats, the silent treatments, and the smashed plates.

But here's the truth no one likes to talk about. **When someone destroys your property as a way to frighten or control you, it's abuse.** You don't have to be physically struck to feel the impact. In many ways, property destruction is designed to send a message without ever touching you:

- I am willing to cross a line.
- I can take away what you love.
- I can make you feel small, afraid, and unsure of what I'll do next.

When that happens, the object that was broken is only the surface level casualty. The real harm settles deeper, into your sense of safety, your trust, and your peace of mind.

The Hidden Logic of Property Destruction

You might wonder why someone would hurt something instead of someone. Sometimes, it feels safer, for the person lashing out, to break an object rather than strike a person outright. But don't be fooled into thinking this is kindness. **It's still about power.**

Consider these examples:

- Someone smashes a glass against the wall during an argument. You flinch and go quiet, afraid the next target will be you.
- Your partner rips up letters from your family after a fight. You feel cut off from people who love you.
- You come home to find your clothes shredded, your photographs burned, your belongings ruined. And you understand that you are not safe.

It's true that not all acts of breaking things are intentional abuse. Sometimes, a plate breaks in a moment of stress without premeditation. But when destruction happens repeatedly, or when it's targeted at items that matter to you, it's about more than anger. It's about sending a message. **And that message is clear: I control what you get to keep.**

The Emotional Fallout: How Broken Things Break Trust

Does throwing a lamp or tearing up a shirt really leave an emotional scar? Research suggests that it does, and often in ways that surprise people.

A study by Tonkin & Burell (2014) looked at how burglary impacts victims. Even when nothing was taken but property was damaged, people often experienced significant psychological distress, shock, anxiety, insomnia, a sense of being unsafe in their own homes.

Imagine how much more intense that impact is when the person destroying your things is someone you trust.

When you live with someone who breaks your possessions in anger, you learn to second guess your safety. You start to wonder what will trigger the next incident. You walk on eggshells, trying to keep the peace.

Some common responses victims describe include:

- A reduced sense of satisfaction in daily life.
- Feeling constantly "on alert."
- Trouble sleeping.
- A growing reluctance to invite people over or talk about what's happening.
- Self blame for "provoking" the destruction.

Over time, your world shrinks. You become a version of yourself who is smaller, quieter, more careful. *And that is the true damage of property destruction: it doesn't just break things. It breaks trust.*

Financial Costs: The Price of Rage

People often underestimate how expensive it is to be destructive. Think about it. When you ruin a piece of furniture, you don't just lose the item, you also lose time, money, and sometimes your reputation.

Here are a few hidden costs:

- **Replacement expenses.** Even small items add up when you're replacing them over and over.
- **Repair costs**. Some things, like electronics, cars, or appliances, are costly to fix, if they can be fixed at all.
- **Collateral damage**. Smashing a glass of wine might stain the carpet. Punching a wall could damage plumbing or wiring.
- **Coaching and recovery**. Survivors of domestic violence often need

counseling or coaching to process trauma, which comes with its own financial burden.
- **Legal fees.** If the incident escalates into criminal charges or civil suits, the expenses multiply.
- **Property settlements**. If you're divorcing, evidence of destruction can influence how property is divided.

And if you think the legal system is lenient about "just breaking things," think again. Malicious damage carries consequences, sometimes severe ones.

The Legal Perspective: When Broken Objects Become Criminal Evidence

It's easy to assume the law only steps in when someone is physically harmed. But in many jurisdictions, property destruction is recognized as a form of domestic abuse.

Malicious damage is defined as intentionally damaging, destroying, or defacing property to cause distress or exert control (Adamgbo, 2023).

Let's be blunt: the legal system does not care whether you intended to scare someone or just "lost control." The impact is the same, and the consequences can be life changing.

Depending on the severity, you could face:

- Restraining orders.
- Criminal charges.
- Fines.
- Jail time.
- Loss of custody or visitation rights.

And the law makes no exception for whether the property was shared or solely owned by the victim (Townsend, Tomaio & Newmark, LLC, 2019).

Here's a sobering reminder: **When you destroy what belongs to someone you love, you're not only damaging a thing, you're crossing a legal and moral line that can be very hard to uncross.**

Examples and Real Life Scenarios

Dion's new neighbors are two men, Martin and Rico who use their apartment as a bachelor pad with their wives and families living a mile from the property. Dion despises the pair since they like to take his favorite parking spot. They are also messy, often leaving their trash stinking up the corridor of their apartment building. On days when Dion arrives late from work, he starts making a habit of taking out his anger on their property. He squeezed his car into his spot, even when it left a nasty mark on the side of Rico's new Civic. He pushed their over filled trash can to the front of their doorstep, so they would have to deal with its stink instead of him and the other neighbors. In addition to these offenses, he made several other bad decisions affecting their property and possessions. He also crumples up Martin's mail. While his actions convey his distaste for Martin and Rico, they hardly do anything communicative or confrontational. Instead, it ends up with them suing him for property damage and vandalism. He has to pay repairs for the damaged car and costs relating to the mail that he tampered with.

Damon and Olivia have been married for a decade. They share a large home and have been paying their landlord for an extended period. They have a shared tenant agreement with both of their names on the leasing document. Only Olivia tends to forget this little detail in her fits of rage. She pulls out the shower holder and things straight off the wall. Her anger leaves dirty scuff marks behind the dinner table. After a particularly tense argument one night, she burns a hole through a desk, which she uses as her work counter.

Even though the house had been remodeled when they first moved in, the couple had to pay several thousand dollars in repairs before they moved out for their divorce. Although Olivia had once acted on her whims, assuming that Damon would have to bear the entirety of the costs of repairs, she had to pay up for half the damages incurred upon the property. The sum amounted to over 10,000 dollars.

How Property Destruction Becomes a Pattern

Rarely does someone wake up and decide to start breaking things.

Usually, it starts with a single outburst, a slammed door, a thrown object, and a quick apology: "I'm sorry, I was just upset. It won't happen again."

And for a while, it doesn't. But eventually, the stress builds up, and the cycle repeats. Each time, the threshold gets lower. Each time, it becomes easier to justify. I've heard countless clients say: **"I never thought I would be the kind of person who did this."**

But when you don't learn healthier ways to cope with anger, the habit grows. And the longer it goes unaddressed, the more destructive it becomes, not only to your relationships but to your sense of self.

Why Some People Use Property to Express Power

If you're reading this and feeling defensive, if you're thinking, "I wasn't trying to hurt anyone!" pause for a moment.

Ask yourself:

- *Why did I feel the need to break something?*
- *What did I want the other person to feel when I did it?*
- *Did it work? And at what cost?*

The truth is, property destruction is almost never about the object. Don't forget, it's about power. About making sure the other person knows you can cross lines if you want to.

Sometimes, it comes from fear, fear of losing control, fear of being rejected. Other times, it's a learned behavior modeled by parents or caregivers who expressed anger in the same way. But no matter where it comes from, it's a behavior you can unlearn.

Preventing Destruction: Learning Different Choices

You don't have to keep repeating this cycle. You can learn to interrupt the pattern before it spirals into another shattered plate, another dented wall, another night you regret.

Here are a few practices to begin:

- **Pause and breathe.** When you feel the urge to lash out, step away. Count backward from 100. Give your body a chance to come down from fight or flight.
- **Name your feeling.** Instead of saying "I'm furious," try "I feel disrespected," or "I feel scared." Naming the real emotion takes away some of its power.
- **Write it out.** Journaling helps you see the thoughts driving your anger.
- **Reframe your interpretation.** If you think, "They don't care about me," ask yourself if that's the only explanation. Maybe they were distracted or overwhelmed themselves.
- **Seek help.** Coaching, anger management classes, and support groups can teach you strategies you might never have learned growing up.

Remember: anger itself isn't wrong. It's what you do with it that matters.

Moving Forward Without Breaking More

If you've been the person who destroys things, this chapter isn't here to shame you. It's here to hold up a mirror so you can see the truth, and decide what you want to do next.

It's possible to change. It's possible to learn a different way. And if you've been the person living in a house where your belongings never feel safe, I want you to hear this: **It wasn't your fault. It isn't your job to fix someone else's rage. And you deserve a life where your things, and your spirit, are respected.**

In the next chapter, we'll explore the quiet erosion of love that happens when one person consistently **Devalues Their Partner's Contributions.**

You've already taken the first step by reading this far. Keep going!!!

VI

-E.W. Howe

"The greatest humiliation in life is to work hard on something from which you expect great appreciation and then fail to get it."

5

Devaluing Your Partner's Contribution to the Relationship

The Subtle Bruises No One Sees

Sometimes, the wounds that hurt the most are the ones nobody else notices. They're hidden in the small, everyday moments when your worth is quietly chipped away.

Maybe you've felt this yourself: that slow erosion of your confidence when every effort you make is brushed aside. The dinner you cooked dismissed as "nothing special." The hours you poured into a project met with a shrug. The way you care, overlooked like it doesn't count at all.

Or maybe you've been the one doing the dismissing. Maybe you didn't realize how often your sighs or silences said, You don't matter. How often your impatience whispered, You're never enough. The truth is, most people don't set out to devalue the person they love. But when stress, resentment, or unspoken disappointment takes over, it's surprisingly easy to forget that someone else's contributions deserve respect, even when you're hurting.

It's tempting to believe that if you aren't screaming or slamming doors, you're not doing any harm. But neglect, sarcasm, and chronic disregard can wound just as deeply as overt cruelty. Devaluation doesn't always announce itself in bold letters. It often slips in quietly, making itself at home in your routines and your tone, until both of you are living inside an atmosphere of disapproval.

Before you can change this dynamic, you have to be willing to see it for what it is. You have to be honest about the ways you've either been diminished, or done the diminishing. That's where healing begins, in naming the harm without sugarcoating it.

What Devaluation Really Looks Like

Let's start with **clarity.** Devaluation isn't simply feeling annoyed or dissatisfied. It's the ongoing pattern of reducing someone's worth in your mind, and then treating them accordingly. You might think of it as the opposite of appreciation. **Where appreciation says: I see what you bring to this relationship. I value you. Devaluation insists: What you do doesn't count. Who you are isn't enough.**

This can sound dramatic when you read it on the page. But in practice, it often looks so ordinary that people barely recognize it:

- The partner who rolls their eyes every time you share an idea.
- The spouse who never says thank you because "that's just your job."
- The friend who only notices what you do wrong but never acknowledges what you do right.

On the surface, it might seem like these moments don't matter much. But over time, they add up. They send a message so consistent that you start to believe it: that your effort, your care, your existence, is somehow lacking.

Psychologist Dr. Ronald Cohen (2023) describes devaluation as a state of exaggerated negativity, where every aspect of someone's behavior is filtered through a critical lens. And once you start seeing a person this way, it's hard to stop. The brain, always eager to confirm its beliefs, keeps hunting for evidence that you're right to be disappointed.

Even if you started out seeing your partner as wonderful, over time, unaddressed resentment can warp that view into something unrecognizable. It's how someone goes from idealization, thinking the other person is perfect, to devaluation, believing they're worthless. This isn't just an abstract concept. In studies of relationships affected by abuse, this swing from all good to all bad is a hallmark of toxic dynamics (Drescher, 2023).

How It Begins: The Cycle of Idealization and Devaluation

If you've ever been swept off your feet by someone who seemed impossibly perfect, you know how intoxicating idealization can be.

At first, it feels like magic. You're convinced this person is everything you've ever wanted. They can do no wrong. Their flaws, if you even notice them, seem charming. **But here's the problem with putting someone on a pedestal: it never lasts.**

People are human. Sooner or later, they disappoint us. They forget an anniversary. They disagree with us. They reveal sides of themselves we didn't expect. And if you haven't learned how to make room for imperfection, the fall from grace can feel catastrophic.

This is often when devaluation starts. The same person who once seemed like a dream now looks like a disappointment. Where you once praised their independence, now you criticize their distance. Where you adored their ambition, now you resent how much time they spend working. **The very qualities that drew you in become the reasons you**

feel let down.

Drescher (2023) explains that this shift is fueled by unrealistic expectations. When we idealize, we create a fantasy version of someone that no real human could sustain. So when reality sets in, we don't just feel ordinary disappointment, we feel betrayed. And instead of grieving the loss of our illusion, we punish the person for not measuring up.

This is how devaluation becomes a cycle. You swing between extremes, first adoration, then disdain, without ever pausing in the middle long enough to see the person clearly.

Recognizing the Forms of Devaluation

Devaluation can show up in dozens of ways. Some are obvious. Others are more diabolical.

But every form sends the same core message, you aren't worthy of respect.

Let's look at a few examples to help you recognize the patterns in your own life:

Emotional and Psychological Devaluation

This is when someone's feelings, thoughts, or needs are routinely dismissed or belittled.

Examples include:

- **Weaponizing insecurities:** Using private vulnerabilities against them in arguments.
- **The silent treatment:** Withdrawing affection or communication as punishment.

These tactics don't just create momentary discomfort. Over time, they erode trust and self esteem, leaving the other person questioning their own reality.

Physical and Material Devaluation

Here, the focus shifts to dismissing tangible contributions.

For example:

- A partner who says, "You don't really do anything around here," ignoring all the care giving or financial support provided.
- A friend who acts as if your generosity, driving them to appointments, helping with bills, doesn't matter.

It's not just hurtful, it's a way of rewriting the narrative so that your effort becomes invisible.

Social and Relational Devaluation

This happens when someone acts as though your value depends entirely on your role in their life.

Examples are:

- Discouraging your friendships.
- Minimizing your achievements outside the relationship.
- Suggesting you have no worth independent of them.

Verbal and Nonverbal Devaluation

Words can wound. So can gestures.

Examples consist of:

- Constant sarcasm or mockery.
- Public criticism disguised as "teasing."
- Eye rolling, sighing, or walking away mid sentence.

Even when nothing is said out loud, nonverbal contempt can land like a slap (Pace, 2021).

The Impact: What Happens to the Person on the Receiving End

I've sat with clients who spent years living in this fog of devaluation. Some came in certain they were "too sensitive." Others insisted they must be imagining things. But here's the truth: if someone constantly makes you feel lesser, it's not your imagination.

Devaluation leaves a mark. And it shows up in three main ways:

- **Emotional Fallout**

Being repeatedly dismissed can lead to profound self doubt. You start believing that maybe you really are unworthy. Your confidence shrinks. Your sense of identity erodes. It can feel like you're nothing without their approval, and that you never quite measure up.

- **Psychological Consequences**

Over time, chronic invalidation can fuel anxiety, depression, and even PTSD. Victims often describe feeling "on edge," never sure what small thing will provoke criticism next. The psychological load is exhausting: you're constantly monitoring yourself, trying not to give them fresh ammunition (Wakefield, 2023; Fletcher & Sissons, n.d.).

- **Physical Toll**

Long term stress doesn't stay in your head. It settles into your body as muscle tension, headaches, fatigue, and illness. Your immune system weakens. You may find yourself sick more often or unable to sleep through the night. No matter how much you try to tell yourself "it's not that bad," your body knows the truth.

How Devaluation Warps Relationship Dynamics

Devaluation isn't just harmful to the person on the receiving end. It also poisons the bond you once shared. When someone's contributions are routinely dismissed, trust evaporates. The relationship stops feeling like a safe place to land. Instead of mutual respect, you get a hierarchy, one person above, the other below.

This power imbalance makes real connection impossible. Over time, the person being devalued may withdraw emotionally or physically. They might stop sharing their thoughts, afraid of being mocked. They may distance themselves to avoid more hurt.

This is how even the closest relationships can disintegrate. Not in a single explosion, but in the slow decay of compassion.

Reclaiming Respect Through Communication

If you've recognized yourself here, either as the one being devalued or the one doing the devaluing, please know this: awareness is the first step to change.

Maybe you didn't mean to hurt each other. Maybe you fell into this pattern because you were overwhelmed or afraid. But you can choose something different now.

Healthy communication is your way out of this cycle. That doesn't mean it's easy. It means you're willing to show up with honesty, humility, and a commitment to do better.

Start with these three principles:

1. **Name It.** Acknowledge what's happening without minimizing it. If you've been hurt, say so. If you've been dismissive, own it.
2. **Listen to Understand.** Not to argue or justify. Not to score points. To understand what it feels like to be on the other side of you.
3. **Validate and Commit.** Validation doesn't mean you agree with every perspective. It means you honor someone's feelings as real. Then commit to new behavior that rebuilds trust.

Moving From Criticism to Appreciation

Even small shifts in how you speak and behave can be transformative.

Here are some ways to practice:

- **Notice the Positive.** Make it a habit to thank your partner for what they do, even the ordinary things.
- **Be Specific.** Instead of vague praise ("You're great"), name exactly

what you value.
- **Catch Yourself.** When you feel irritation bubbling up, pause. Ask yourself, is this really about them, or is this about something in me that needs attention?

Remember, no relationship thrives without appreciation. And no person flourishes when their efforts are invisible.

Moving Forward: Choosing Respect Over Resentment

Sometimes, even after you start communicating differently, old wounds linger. The hurt from years of devaluation doesn't vanish just because you've decided to be kinder. It takes time. Repetition. Trust rebuilt in small, consistent moments.

No matter how long you've been stuck in the cycle, it's never too late to choose respect over resentment, connection over contempt. The path forward is built one conversation, one acknowledgment, one act of appreciation at a time.

In the next chapter, **Disregarding Your Feelings**, we'll explore how to honor not just your partner's contributions, but also their heart, and why disregarding them can be just as damaging as devaluing their efforts.

VII

— Maya Angelou

"People will forget what you said, people will forget what you did, but people will never forget how you made them feel."

6

Disregarding Your Feelings

Your Feelings Are Not The Enemy

Have you ever sat across from someone you love, someone you trust and felt like you were speaking into a void?

You can feel the words leaving your lips, but they seem to land nowhere. No recognition. No softening of the eyes. No nod of understanding.

It's a peculiar loneliness, isn't it? Being right next to another human and feeling completely unseen.

Maybe you've been on the receiving end of this, feeling as if your heart is speaking a language the other person refuses to learn. Or maybe, if you're honest, you've been the one crossing your arms, dismissing a partner's quiet plea to be heard.

It can be easy to convince ourselves that simply showing up, sitting at the same dinner table, exchanging polite "how was your day?", is enough. But real connection demands more. It asks us to recognize that feelings are facts, even if we don't understand them or agree with them.

In my years of working with couples and individuals navigating the

fallout of emotional disregard, I've learned this: feeling invisible in a relationship is one of the most painful experiences a person can have. It erodes trust. It hollows out the bond that was meant to be a refuge. It leaves people questioning their worth and their sanity.

And yet, it's also astonishingly common.

Let's explore how this happens, how the subtle, almost unnoticeable habit of disregarding another person's feelings can quietly dismantle intimacy. And how you can rebuild respect, as well as, understanding if this dynamic has taken root in your own life.

What Emotional Disregard Really Means

We throw around words like "neglect" or "disrespect," but what does emotional disregard actually look like?

At its core, emotional disregard is the pattern of consistently minimizing, dismissing, or ignoring another person's feelings. You might not set out to hurt them. You might think you're simply being rational or practical. But over time, your unwillingness to acknowledge their emotional experience tells them they don't matter.

Dr. Shafir (2022) defines emotional disregard as the absence of love, validation, and appreciation in close relationships. It's the moment when someone says, *"I'm hurting,"* and you look away, change the subject, or sigh in irritation.

It can happen in hundreds of small, ordinary moments:

When your partner shares something vulnerable, and you tease them for being "dramatic." When your child expresses sadness, and you briskly say, *"You're fine. It's not a big deal."* When a friend confides their anxiety, and you respond with, "Just get over it."

These reactions might seem harmless in isolation. But repeated over weeks, months, or years, they build a wall between you.

I've worked with many people who could recite every time their

feelings were brushed aside. They remembered the exact words, the tone, even the way their partner's eyes glazed over.

Because when your feelings are repeatedly disregarded, it doesn't just hurt in the moment. It teaches you that your emotions are burdensome. It conditions you to hide what you feel, to stop reaching out.

And eventually, it convinces you that love means being invisible.

Examples and Scenarios

Shoni spends her last paycheck purchasing an expensive wallet for her boyfriend, Aaron. She surprises him on his birthday at an expensive restaurant with their friends. Aaron picks up the present, only to scoff and say, "Did you get this at a discount? I can't believe you thought I would like this! It's so tacky!" While Aaron may have considered the wallet to be tacky, Shoni spent time and money on it so that he could enjoy it. She must have considered herself worthy because she had planned to surprise him with the gift. By insulting Shoni's choices in front of their friends, Aaron humiliates Shoni and disregards the efforts she has put into their relationship.

Jerry and Joseph have been friends for a long time. They like giving each other thoughtful presents on birthdays, a tradition they have upheld for several years. On one birthday, Jerry gets Joseph an autographed copy of his favorite book. Upon receiving the gift, Joseph remarks, "You sure like showing off how much richer you are than I am, don't you?" Criticizing Jerry's act of kindness, as a show of wealth makes the positive act of gifting into a negative experience. Jerry feels belittled for the efforts.

Jennifer and Dave are married. Dave struggles to find footing between his two jobs, one of which is physically demanding. Jennifer understands that Dave is exhausted by these jobs' toll on him. However, she refuses to compromise about the expectations she chooses to place on him in their marriage. She defines a successful marriage as the sum of expensive clothing and other personal belongings. Even when Dave submits to these requirements, she ridicules him for not putting more effort into their relationship. She dismisses the hardship Dave must undergo at his job. Still, she expects him to be unaffected by her constantly picking at him. Her behavior leaves her husband feeling emotionally exhausted, and at a loss for how he must go about things in the future. The relationship, therefore, becomes a primary source of stress and tension in his life.

The Subtle Ways Emotional Disregard Shows Up

Most people don't set out to invalidate their loved ones. It usually begins as a defense mechanism, a way to avoid uncomfortable conversations or keep from feeling overwhelmed by someone else's needs. But over time, this pattern can become habitual.

Here are some of the most common forms of emotional disregard:

- **Minimizing or trivializing feelings.** When someone says, "That's nothing," or, "You're overreacting," it sends the message that your emotions are exaggerated or unimportant.
- **Criticizing vulnerability.** Teasing or mocking a person for crying or expressing fear reinforces shame about their emotional needs.
- **Emotional stonewalling.** Shutting down or walking away when someone is upset can feel like punishment, leaving the other person feeling abandoned in their distress.
- **Withholding affection or reassurance.** Refusing to offer comfort after conflict creates an environment where connection feels conditional.
- **Perpetual indifference.** Consistently responding with apathy, even to significant experiences or milestones, conveys that nothing really moves you.
- **Invalidating perspective.** Telling someone their experience is

"wrong" or "ridiculous" instead of trying to understand where they're coming from.

Shafir (2022) describes these behaviors as relational toxins. They don't always look dramatic from the outside, but over time they corrode the trust and closeness that healthy relationships require.

Why We Dismiss Feelings (Even When We Care)

If you grew up in an environment where emotions were brushed aside or shamed, you probably learned early on that vulnerability was dangerous. Maybe you were taught that feelings are weaknesses to be conquered. Maybe your caretakers simply didn't have the skills to validate you.

And so, as an adult, you might find yourself replicating what you knew, even when you don't want to.

You might be uncomfortable with strong displays of emotion, fearing they'll spiral into chaos. You might be so consumed by your own stress that someone else's feelings feel like too much. Or you might believe that responding practically, "Here's how to fix it," is more helpful than offering empathy.

In reality, what most people long for isn't a solution. It's to be met with understanding. When someone says, "I feel like you don't care," our instinct is often to defend ourselves, "Of course I care. You're overreacting." But from their perspective, the lack of validation feels exactly like indifference.

It takes humility to pause and consider that your good intentions aren't always experienced as care.

The Impact of Emotional Disregard

Sometimes people ask me, "But is this really abuse? I'm not yelling or calling names."

No, emotional disregard doesn't always rise to the level of overt abuse. But that doesn't mean it isn't harmful.

Psychologist Lindsay Gibson writes about "emotional neglect" as an invisible wound that can shape how a person relates to themselves and the world.

Research consistently shows that chronic invalidation can lead to:

- Depression
- Anxiety disorders
- Emotional numbness
- Poor self esteem
- Difficulty trusting others

When someone you love repeatedly dismisses your feelings, you start to believe there's something wrong with you for having them.

I've seen clients who, after years of emotional disregard, can no longer identify what they feel. When I ask, "How does that make you feel?" they look at me blankly, unsure how to answer.

This is because emotional invalidation conditions you to disconnect from your own experience. It teaches you that to be safe, or loved, you must silence yourself.

And that, in my opinion, is one of the greatest tragedies of all.

How to Rebuild Emotional Connection

The good news is that emotional disregard isn't irreversible. If you recognize these patterns in yourself, or in your relationship, you can learn new ways to show up.

Here are some guiding principles to help you begin:

1. Listen to understand, not to fix
Most of us are wired to jump into problem solving mode the second we hear distress. It feels practical, even loving. But more often than not, what the other person really needs isn't a solution, it's to feel heard.

When someone shares something vulnerable, practice slowing down your instinct to respond with advice. Instead, offer your presence.

Try saying:

- *"That sounds really painful. Tell me more."*
- *"I hear you."*
- *"I can see why you'd feel that way."*

These simple words can be surprisingly powerful. They create a space where feelings are safe to exist.

2. Validate Their Perspective
Validation doesn't mean you agree with everything they say. It means you respect that their experience is real to them.

When you respond with disbelief or dismissal, "That's ridiculous," "You're too sensitive," you're effectively telling them their reality doesn't count.

Instead, try:

- *"I see that this really affected you."*
- *"It makes sense you'd feel upset."*

Validation is the opposite of defensiveness. It's saying: I care enough to step into your world, even when it's uncomfortable.

3. Re evaluate Expectations

One of the biggest reasons we disregard feelings is because we're carrying unrealistic expectations, of ourselves and the people we love.

Ask yourself honestly:

- Am I expecting them to meet all my emotional needs?
- Am I assuming they should never need anything from me?
- Am I withholding care because they didn't act exactly as I hoped?

Healthy relationships are built on mutual support and realistic boundaries. No one can be your sole source of fulfillment, and you shouldn't have to be someone else's, either.

4. Practice Emotional Attunement

Emotional attunement is the art of noticing what isn't said.

It's paying attention to the shift in someone's tone. The way their shoulders slump. The silence that feels heavier than usual. When you sense something is off, gently check in.

Try asking:

"You seem quiet. Is something on your mind?"

This doesn't just show you care. It also lets the other person know they matter enough for you to notice their inner world.

5. Be Patient with Yourself

Unlearning old habits takes time. If you've spent years deflecting feelings or shutting down, you won't become emotionally attuned overnight.

You will slip up. You'll catch yourself defaulting to minimization or avoidance. That doesn't mean you're failing.

When it happens:

- Pause.
- Apologize without excuses.
- Try again.

Progress isn't about being perfect. It's about showing up, over and over, even when it's messy.

Preventing Emotional Disregard

One of the most powerful antidotes to emotional disregard is cultivating **emotional intelligence.**

According to Cherry (2024), emotional intelligence has three core components:

1. **Self awareness.** Recognizing your own emotions as they arise.
2. **Empathy.** Understanding and feeling what others feel.
3. **Regulation.** Managing your reactions in ways that honor both your feelings and theirs.

By practicing these skills, you don't just improve your relationships, you become someone who makes others feel safe, valued, and seen.

Moving Forward: Your Feelings Matter

If you recognize yourself in these pages, if you've hurt someone you love by disregarding their feelings, know this: You are not beyond redemption.

Awareness is the beginning of change. Each time you choose to listen instead of dismiss, to validate instead of criticize, to stay present instead of shutting down, you are building something stronger and more genuine.

And if you are the person whose feelings have been disregarded, please hear this: Your emotions matter. You deserve to be met with curiosity, respect, and care.

Healing is possible, for both of you.

In the next chapter, we'll explore **Discontentment Towards Your Partner's Gestures**, and how to break free from the habits that keep you from receiving love in all its forms.

VIII

— Socrates

"He who is not contented with what he has, would not be contented with what he would like to have."

7

Discontentment Towards Your Partner's Gestures

When Everything Seems Fine, But Feels Empty

Have you ever looked around at your life, at the person you share it with, at the comforts you've built together, and still felt an unsettling emptiness you couldn't name? Maybe you're the one providing, showing up, doing all the right things. Or maybe you're on the receiving end of countless little gestures meant to show love, dinners cooked, shoulders rubbed, bills paid, yet there's a dull ache inside you whispering, This isn't enough.

I've sat across from people who spent years trying to rationalize that voice away. They'd tell themselves, *I should be grateful, I'm being selfish, maybe I'm just hard to please.* But no amount of scolding or pretending can quiet the discontent that blooms when needs go unspoken or unacknowledged.

And sometimes, it's not your own dissatisfaction you're wrestling with, it's the heaviness of a partner who seems perpetually unimpressed. You see their glazed over expression when you try to connect, or hear the sigh in their voice when you offer something you hoped would make them feel loved. It's a strange kind of loneliness, being together yet feeling perpetually unseen.

Discontentment isn't always about greed or unrealistic expectations. More often, it's about longing, for understanding, for reciprocity, for a deeper sense of belonging. And if left unaddressed, it can hollow out even the most promising relationship.

This chapter is an invitation to look at discontentment without judgment or shame. To see it as a signal rather than a failure. And to learn how you can cultivate a culture of appreciation that bridges the gaps between you.

Understanding Discontentment

Discontentment in a relationship doesn't announce itself loudly at first. It often starts as a subtle tension, a sense that something is missing, even when everything looks fine on the surface. You might catch yourself thinking, "Why do I feel restless when my life is technically good?"

This feeling is more common than most people admit. Studies show that dissatisfaction often arises from **cognitive distortions**, automatic thoughts that twist reality in ways that magnify negativity and diminish gratitude (Identifying Cognitive Distortions in Relationships, 2023).

You may not realize it, but you could be carrying unconscious beliefs such as:

- If my partner really loved me, they'd know exactly what I need without me asking.
- If there's conflict, it must mean this relationship isn't right.
- If my partner can't fulfill every expectation, I'm settling.

These patterns can turn everyday imperfections into proof that you're missing out or being shortchanged.

Discontentment also grows when comparison becomes a habit. The highlight reels you see on social media, smiling selfies, romantic vacations, effortless affection, can feed the belief that your relationship is deficient.

In reality, the ordinary gestures your partner offers, brewing your coffee, folding your laundry, asking how your day was, often mean more than any grand display you envy from afar. But when discontentment takes root, those gestures can feel invisible.

Signs You or Your Partner Are Struggling

Discontentment rarely stays hidden forever. Over time, it leaves a trail of behaviors and feelings that change the temperature of your connection.

Here are some common signs that discontentment might be simmering under the surface:

- You or your partner feel unsupported or unvalidated.
- Minor disagreements escalate into full blown arguments.
- There's frequent criticism or second guessing of each other's decisions.
- One or both of you begin to undervalue the contributions you each make.
- One partner starts to interfere more, correcting, controlling, or micromanaging (Papa Pintor, 2017).

If any of these resonate with you, take a breath. It doesn't mean you're doomed. It means you're human. And it means something in your relationship is asking for attention.

Examples and Scenarios

April has been with her boyfriend, Rob, for three years. They live together in an apartment and consider themselves on the path to marriage. However, April can't help but feel she's missing out on life by committing to another person at a young age. When she's with Rob at clubs and parties, she wonders what her experiences would be like if she were alone in the same places. Her thinking makes her miss the days when she was single, going out with friends without having to check in with Rob. Ironically, Rob would not have minded her exploring these relationships herself. Her fear of communicating her dissatisfaction in the relationship only causes a breach in the trust that they have built together. Eventually, Rob and April dissolve their relationship because they cannot figure out why they feel so distant from each other.

Carl and Felecia have just moved several thousands of miles away from their friends and family for a work opportunity. Carl has been promoted to a high position at a foreign branch of the company where he works, with his pay increasing to twice the amount he had been making at home. Felecia is happy for him. She works from home in their new apartment, using her evenings to make friends with the community of ex patriots she finds living close by. Since Carl works longer hours, Felecia takes charge of weekday cooking and laundry. Carl sees this yet has an inkling of doubt and insecurity about how fulfilling their relationship is. He can't help but compare his marriage to the relationships he observes at work, with partners raking up likes on social media with their public displays of affection for each other. The issue is that Felecia is a private person who isn't interested in posting much about Carl on social media. He soon starts to compare Felecia to his friends' partners, often picking on every little fault so that he can tell her how much better other people seem to be living their lives. This hurts Felecia deeply, as she is putting in genuine effort for Carl and doesn't appreciate being invalidated by him. In short, the frictions and arguments become more than either can handle, and they divorce.

How Discontentment Impacts the One on the Receiving End

When you're the person offering effort and care only to feel that it falls flat, it can be devastating. Imagine working late to afford a small getaway you thought your partner would love, only to hear, It's not really what I had in mind. Or putting your heart into a gesture, like cooking their favorite meal, only to be met with a distracted nod.

Over time, this chips away at your spirit. You might start to wonder:

- Am I not enough?
- Is something wrong with me?
- Will I ever be appreciated for who I am?

The emotional fallout can look like:

- **Withdrawal.** You stop trying as hard because nothing seems to make a difference.
- **Frustration.** You feel irritable and resentful that your efforts go unnoticed.
- **Negativity.** Pessimism creeps into other parts of your life.
- **Reduced intimacy.** Vulnerability feels unsafe when you expect disappointment.
- **Escapism.** You distract yourself with work, hobbies, or other relationships to numb the ache (Gupta, n.d.).

One client once described it perfectly: *"It feels like living in a house where every light is burnt out. You can still find your way around, but you can't see the warmth anymore."*

Why Appreciation Is Non Negotiable

If discontentment is the slow erosion of goodwill, appreciation is the steady repair of the foundation. **Appreciation doesn't mean ignoring flaws or pretending everything is perfect. It means seeing your partner's efforts, even when they fall short of your ideal.** It means acknowledging that love is expressed in a hundred small, imperfect ways.

Think about the everyday ways your partner contributes:

- They make sure your car has gas.
- They walk the dog in the rain.
- They leave the porch light on when you're late.

These acts might feel mundane, but they're the scaffolding that holds your life together. When you stop seeing them, resentment finds space to grow.

Research shows that couples who regularly express gratitude feel closer, fight less, and report higher satisfaction over time (Algoe, 2012). **Appreciation is like oxygen, relationships can survive brief lapses without it, but eventually, the absence becomes suffocating.**

Rebuilding Appreciation and Connection

If you're realizing you've become critical or hard to please, that doesn't make you a bad partner. It makes you a partner who's ready to grow.

Here are some gentle, practical ways to invite more appreciation back into your relationship:

Reflect Before Reacting
When you feel the urge to criticize or dismiss, pause. Ask yourself:

- What need is going unmet right now?
- Is this about the present moment, or is something older being stirred up?

Often, discontentment is more about what you're longing for than what your partner is failing to provide.

Express Gratitude Regularly
It sounds simple, but saying thank you sincerely can transform the emotional climate between you.

Try this:

- Before bed, name one thing you noticed and appreciated that day.
- Leave a note or send a text expressing gratitude.
- Offer praise in front of others, nothing feels quite as validating as being publicly appreciated.

Make Time for Quality Connection
Busyness is the silent killer of appreciation. When you're always rushing, you stop noticing the good. Block out time to simply be together. This might look like:

- A weekly date night, no phones allowed.
- A walk after dinner to catch up.
- A quiet morning with coffee and no agenda.

The point isn't what you do, it's that you do it together.

Practice Receiving Without Judgment

If you tend to minimize or brush off your partner's gestures, practice letting them land. When they offer something, a compliment, a hug, a small gift, pause. Feel it. Say thank you without qualifiers like, You didn't have to do that. Your acceptance is a gift in return.

Communicate Your Needs Kindly

Discontentment often festers because needs stay hidden. You're allowed to ask for what nourishes you. Just be sure to frame it in a way that invites connection rather than blame.

For example:

- Instead of: *You never do anything romantic.*
- Try: *I'd love if we planned something special together soon. It helps me feel close to you.*

Preventing Discontentment Going Forward

Once you start cultivating appreciation, you'll probably notice it doesn't erase every frustration. That's okay. **Gratitude isn't about denying what's hard, it's about balancing it with what's good.**

Here are a few reminders to help you stay anchored:

- **Progress is gradual.** Just because you're making changes doesn't mean your partner will immediately respond. Keep showing up.
- **Resist the comparison trap.** Social media is not real life. Your love doesn't have to look like anyone else's.
- **Let go of perfection.** A healthy relationship is two imperfect people choosing each other, again and again.

Whenever you feel yourself drifting into discontent, come back to this question: What am I grateful for today? Even the smallest answer can steady you.

Moving Forward: Choosing Appreciation

If you take only one idea from this chapter, let it be this: ***Appreciation is a practice.*** It's not something you either have or don't. It's something you cultivate, through noticing, naming, and cherishing what's already here.

No one can do this work for you. And no one can take away the peace that comes when you learn to love your life exactly as it is, even as you hope for more. Remember, it's never too late to choose gratitude over grievance. To see what is good. To say thank you. And to mean it.

In the next chapter, we'll talk about **Dysfunctionality Within Your Relationship**, how old wounds, unhelpful patterns, and unspoken expectations can create cycles of hurt, and how you can begin to untangle them.

IX

—Karen Salmansohn

"Dysfunctional relationships are a lot like a bad habit—hard to break, comforting in their familiarity, and destructive in the long run."

8

Dysfunctionality Within Your Relationship

Dysfunctionality Anyone?

It starts as little things you brush aside. The tension after an argument. The way you stop sharing stories over dinner. The feeling that you're never fully safe to be yourself. Over time, these seemingly small fractures grow into chasms, gaps so wide you barely recognize your relationship anymore.

Dysfunctionality is a word that sounds clinical and detached. But in practice, it's anything but distant. It's the knot in your stomach when your partner walks into the room. It's the exhaustion of fighting the same battles over and over, with no end in sight. **Dysfunction happens when a relationship strays so far from its purpose, love, safety, respect, that it becomes a source of suffering.**

Contrary to what romantic movies might have you believe, no relationship is always smooth. Every couple struggles, disagrees, and disappoints each other sometimes. But when you spend more time feeling wounded, small, or unsafe than you do feeling valued, dysfunction has likely taken hold.

In fact, some therapists offer a simple benchmark: if only 20% of your time together feels positive, and the other 80% feels stressful or combative, you're not in a healthy relationship (Beer Becker, 2022).

If this resonates with you, you are not alone, and you are not doomed. But you do need to pause and look honestly at what's happening. The patterns you tolerate today will shape your tomorrow.

Recognizing the Signs of Dysfunction

Dysfunction doesn't always announce itself with slammed doors or public fights. Often, it's a slow erosion, tiny cracks in trust, respect, or empathy. Over time, these patterns harden into the culture of your relationship.

Here are some of the most common signs of dysfunction:

- **Extreme Dominance or Submission** Relationships thrive on balance. If one partner always controls decisions, or if one partner always yields, that power imbalance breeds resentment and fear. Over time, it can crush your sense of self.
- **Constant Accusations and Blame** When blame becomes the main form of communication, trust evaporates. You might feel like you're always defending yourself instead of connecting.
- **Grudges and Resentment** Everyone makes mistakes. But using old failures as ammunition poisons even the best intentions. If every disagreement turns into a rehashing of past hurts, the relationship can't move forward.
- **Poor Boundaries** Healthy intimacy doesn't mean losing your individuality. If you feel pressured to share everything, surrender your privacy, or be constantly available, your boundaries have been compromised.

- **Lack of Emotional Availability** You need more than a warm body beside you. You deserve someone who will sit with your sadness, cheer for your hopes, and honor your humanity. Without emotional presence, connection withers.
- **Disloyalty** Criticizing your partner behind their back or violating their trust by cheating is among the most painful breaches. These acts of disloyalty tear at the foundation of love itself (Beer Becker, 2022; Marriage.com Editorial Team, 2021).

Each of these signs doesn't just hurt in the moment. They create cycles of insecurity and fear that become the air you breathe.

Why Dysfunction Takes Root

It's easy to believe dysfunction is the fault of one "bad" partner or a sign of an irreparably broken relationship. But the truth is often more complicated. Many of the behaviors that damage our connections started as survival strategies.

Some psychologists refer to these patterns as "dances" (Buffalmano, 2021). The moves might look different, withdrawal, criticism, control, but they all grow out of old fears and learned roles.

Maybe your family of origin taught you to equate love with control. Perhaps you watched your caregivers ignore or belittle each other. Maybe you internalized that to be safe, you had to be perfect, or invisible.

Children absorb everything. If you grew up surrounded by unpredictable tempers or emotional distance, you likely developed ways to cope that now play out in your adult relationships. You may default to appeasing, stonewalling, or attacking because those habits once protected you. Today, they're harming you.

This doesn't mean you're broken. It means you're human.

Common Dysfunctional Dynamics

Not every relationship fits neatly into a category, but reflecting on these familiar patterns can help you spot your own "dance."

- **The Parent and the Child** One partner assumes responsibility, rules, and judgment. The other becomes the carefree rebel. At first, this may feel complementary, but over time it often breeds resentment. The "parent" grows exhausted, the "child" feels infantilized.
- **The Authority and the Rebel** One partner enforces rigid standards, while the other resists through secretive behavior or passive defiance. Trust erodes, leaving each person feeling misunderstood.
- **The Demander and the Withdrawer** The Demander seeks reassurance but does so with criticism and neediness. The Withdrawer retreats, overwhelmed. The more one pushes, the more the other pulls away.
- **The Boxer and the Avoider** One partner thrives on confrontation, while the other fears it. This dynamic keeps intimacy at bay, cycling between eruptions and silence.
- **The Saint and the Sinner** The Saint sees themselves as morally superior, enduring the Sinner's chaos with a martyr's patience. This dynamic often masks co dependency, with neither partner growing.
- **The Reminder and the Forgetful** One partner becomes the taskmaster, carrying the burden of organization. The other shrinks away from accountability. Resentment festers (Buffalmano, 2021).

It can feel sobering to see yourself in these descriptions. But remember: these are not destiny. They're learned patterns, and what's learned can be unlearned.

The Impact of Dysfunction

Living in a dysfunctional relationship doesn't just make you unhappy. It reshapes how you see yourself, your partner, and the world.

Many people experience:

- **A Sense of Powerlessness** You may feel stuck, like no matter what you do, nothing changes. This powerlessness can seep into every area of your life, dimming your ambition and joy.
- **Boundary Confusion** Dysfunction blurs the line between self and other. You might feel overexposed, or, paradoxically, completely alone.
- **Conflict Avoidance or Escalation** Because disagreements never get resolved, conflict becomes something to dread or provoke. Either way, you lose the chance to repair.
- **Loss of Compassion** The longer dysfunction lasts, the harder it becomes to see your partner as anything but an adversary.
- **Eroded Intimacy** When you feel criticized or invisible, vulnerability becomes too risky. Emotional distance grows. Physical connection often suffers too.
- **Belief You're Unworthy** If the person closest to you treats you like you're unlovable, it's only a matter of time before you start believing it (Dysfunctional Relationships | Saprea, 2023).

Examples and Scenarios

Duchess and Steve have only been dating for a year, but Steve feels he's taken her under his wing. For all her life, Duchess had been brought up under the strict watch of her conservative parents. She was barely allowed to go out if she wasn't with her parents or at school. So, when Steve moved out of town for college, she was excited to explore parties and relationships with new acquaintances. She loved every minute of it. After all, she had met Steve at school. He was older than her and more popular. However, Steve was much more reserved about socialization than Duchess proved to be. He thought Duchess needed someone to look out for her, so he insisted on coming with her to most of the social gatherings she took part in. Duchess would not have minded this, except that Steve always held her extroversions above her, as if he was standing on some kind of moral high ground. He criticized her actions and gave her unsolicited advice about how she could have better discipline. He exhausted her and made her feel terrible about herself.

Ebony and Nate are high school sweethearts. They have known each other since they were in kindergarten. The attraction between them had felt obvious when they first got together. Everyone had always expected the two of them to end up together. By the time they graduated from college, they had been living together for nearly two years. All their friends considered them to be a perfect couple. However, sometimes, Nate found himself feeling irrationally angry at Ebony. He didn't like how Ebony liked to control how he went about his day. There would be nights when he would come back home exhausted from work, and Ebony would talk about how he needed to find a way to better their relationship. At times like this, Nate tended to keep quiet. There was no stopping Ebony when she got into her moods. Almost every day, even the spectacularly good ones, would end up with a fight or a discussion about how they could improve. Despite the frequency of these conversations, they hardly ever moved toward concrete solutions for their problems. Ebony never knew what she wanted. Nate only wanted to be left alone with his dog and cigars.

Facing Dysfunction with Honesty

It's tempting to pretend everything is fine. To blame circumstances, or to hope that if you just wait it out, things will get better. But denial only prolongs your pain.

Acknowledging dysfunction doesn't mean you've failed. It means you're finally telling yourself the truth. From that truth, you can begin to heal.

Ask yourself:

- What patterns do you keep repeating, despite knowing they hurt?
- What do you avoid saying because you're afraid of conflict?
- What do you long for that you're too ashamed to name?

This is the work, unearthing what's been buried so you can create something better.

Steps Toward Change

Here are some ways to start building healthier dynamics:

- **Reflect on Your Family Scripts** What did you learn about love growing up? What beliefs did you inherit about control, sacrifice, or worth?
- **Heal Old Wounds** You can't rewrite the past, but you can give yourself compassion. Therapy, coaching, or support groups can help you make sense of formative pain.
- **Practice New Skills** Learn to set boundaries, express needs calmly, and listen without defensiveness. These are muscles that strengthen with use.

- **Be Patient** Patterns formed over decades won't disappear overnight. Celebrate small progress.
- **Take Ownership** You can't control your partner's choices. But you can change how you show up.

Building a Functional Relationship

Healthy relationships don't look perfect. They look like two flawed people committed to growth. They look like honest conversations and forgiveness. Like showing up, again and again, even when it's hard.

Here are practices to consider:

- **Set Shared Goals** Agree on what you both want to change. Aligning your vision fosters teamwork.
- **Have Regular Check Ins** Make time to talk about how you're feeling and what's working.
- **Acknowledge the Good** Gratitude can soften hard edges. Notice what your partner does right.
- **Own Your Impact** When you slip into old patterns, apologize without excuses.
- **Stay Curious** Ask questions. Listen. Remember: you don't know everything about your partner, even after years.
- **Protect Your Joy** Make space for laughter and connection, even in hard seasons.
- **Honor Each Other's Humanity** You are both doing the best you can with what you've learned.

Moving Forward: No More Dysfunction

If you've read this far, you already have something many people don't: awareness. Awareness is the doorway to change.

No matter how tangled your history, you can learn to love differently. It won't happen all at once, and it won't always be easy. But it will be worth it.

Because you deserve a relationship that feels safe, nourishing, and alive.

In the next chapter, we'll explore **Deceiving Your Partner** and how honoring each other can heal connection instead of threatening it.

X

- Stephen King

"The trust of the innocent is the liar's most useful tool."

9

Deceiving Your Partner

A Slippery Slope No One Sets Out to Climb

Have you ever caught yourself telling a small lie, the sort you believed was harmless, a tiny cushion to protect someone you loved from disappointment? Maybe you thought, It's just easier this way. At first, it may have felt like a kindness or a shortcut to avoid conflict. But if you've ever watched that little lie swell into something much larger, something that changed the way your partner looked at you, you already understand how powerful deception can be.

No one walks into a relationship planning to become dishonest. Most of us imagine ourselves as truthful people. We value integrity, especially with the people we trust most. Yet, the reality of being human means that we all, at times, hide, edit, or bend the truth. And when that becomes a pattern, it quietly rewrites the entire story you and your partner thought you were telling together.

This is the quiet heartbreak of deception: it doesn't just betray the other person, it undermines the ground you both stand on. Whether the lie is about something seemingly trivial or something that changes the course of a life, the effect is the same: a slow erosion of trust, the feeling that the person you love is a stranger.

Let's look closely at why deception so often takes hold, why it feels easier in the moment, and how it inevitably does more damage than we first imagine.

What Deception Really Means

Deception isn't always the obvious betrayal of an affair or a major secret. Sometimes, it's the small omissions that slip between two people. It can be the way you avoid answering a question, or the way your body language deflects curiosity. It can be half truths you tell yourself so you can keep telling them to someone else.

Deception is any act, big or small, that intentionally misleads another person (Kapoor, 2023). In relationships, this can take many forms:

- Hiding purchases or financial issues.
- Downplaying interactions with someone else.
- Exaggerating achievements.
- Pretending to feel something you don't.
- Minimizing the seriousness of mistakes.

One of the most insidious forms of deception is pathological lying, a pattern of compulsive falsehoods told without clear purpose. People who lie pathologically often start out trying to protect themselves or preserve an image. Over time, the lies become an almost reflexive habit. What began as occasional self protection turns into chronic dishonesty that corrodes every interaction.

In my work with couples, I've seen how easy it is to slide into this trap. You tell yourself you're sparing your partner's feelings or buying time to sort yourself out. But in reality, you're building a wall brick by brick between you.

According to research, while nearly 90% of adults say infidelity is wrong, between 50% and 60% of married men and 45% to 55% of married women in the U.S. admit to at least one act of cheating (Firestone, 2011). That statistic alone shows how often our ideals of honesty collide with our behavior. It's worth pausing here to recognize that not every person who lies is cruel or malicious.

Many times, deception grows from fear:

- Fear of disappointing the person you love.
- Fear of losing the relationship.
- Fear of revealing who you really are.

But no matter why it happens, deception always leaves a mark.

Why People Lie to Those They Love

People lie for many reasons, and some of them even feel noble in the moment. Here are some of the most common motivations I hear:

- **To avoid conflict.** If telling the truth feels like it will lead to an argument, lying can look like the simpler path.
- **To protect your image.** You don't want your partner to see your flaws, so you curate a version of yourself that looks better.
- **To maintain control.** Information is power. When you control what someone knows, you control how they see you.
- **To avoid consequences.** Sometimes it feels easier to cover up a mistake than face the fallout.
- **To spare someone's feelings.** You convince yourself the truth would

hurt them more than a lie.
- **To feel special.** Small embellishments can become part of an identity you prefer over reality.
- **To resist change.** If you know telling the truth would force you to adjust your life, denial can feel more comfortable (Stritof, n.d.).

I've heard countless clients say, I never meant to hurt them. And often, that's true. But intention doesn't erase the impact. Every time you lie, you trade genuine connection for the illusion of peace. You might avoid a conflict today, but you plant seeds of doubt that will eventually grow into something harder to uproot.

The Impact of Lies on Your Partner

If you've ever been lied to by someone you trusted, you know the feeling: the ground shifts under your feet. Even small lies can leave you questioning what else isn't real.

Repeated deception attacks more than trust, it damages a person's sense of reality. And when the person you count on most keeps rewriting the truth, you start to wonder whether your instincts are trustworthy at all.

Consider the ways your partner may be impacted:

- **Eroded trust:** The more often you lie, the harder it is for your partner to take you at your word.
- **Emotional distance:** It's nearly impossible to feel close to someone whose honesty you doubt.
- **Diminished empathy:** If your partner feels repeatedly deceived, they may stop trying to see your side.
- **Reduced intimacy:** Vulnerability requires safety. And safety requires

truth.
- **Self doubt:** Victims of deception often wonder if they are to blame. They may think, "What did I do to deserve this?"
- **Lasting trauma:** Research shows that repeated dishonesty activates the brain's threat response. Over time, this can create chronic anxiety and make healing much harder (Stritof, n.d.).

When you're the one who lied, it can feel overwhelming to face the hurt you've caused. But understanding this impact is the first step in taking responsibility.

Examples and Scenarios

LaShondra and Charles had only been together for about four months, but the trauma inflicted in the short period of those four months caused LaShondra much pain. Charles had promised LaShondra that he planned to marry her. On the pretext of an upcoming marriage, the two had engaged in premarital sex despite it being strongly frowned upon in their community and culture. In truth, Charles had only planned to use LaShondra for some experience with a woman before marrying his true love. He had manipulated LaShondra's trust to have his way with her. He had pretended she could trust him, often taking the role of her best friend. During their relationship, Charles used deception to manipulate their relationship for his convenience. He would even do things like tell her that he only wanted to meet her to have a discussion, then proceed to coerce her into having sex with him. At best, consent in these events was blurry because Charles often used the pretext of a promised marriage to get what he wanted.

Given that LaShondra was often very shy and introverted, she hardly opened up to anyone who wasn't in her family. She hated how Charles had made her trust him, only to use her and then brag about having his way with her to his friends. Even a year after the course of their relationship,

LaShondra felt traumatized by her experience. She felt ashamed to talk about what she went through with her therapist. She even felt terrified when a date tried to reach for her hand. Essentially, Charles' lying scarred LaShondra.

Ellery and Eleesha love each other. However, Ellery confides in a friend about a week into his marriage about how distrustful he feels towards his wife. Eleesha is everything Ellery had longed for in a long term relationship. She is beautiful, smart, and very kind. Still, Eleesha has a habit of lying that Ellery finds difficult to ignore. In the early stages of their relationship, Eleesha had only lied about little things. She would swear that Ellery had taken responsibility for a grocery order she had forgotten to pick up. Eleesha would also have the craziest, most unrealistic stories about her exes. At the time, Ellery had found it cute. After their marriage, however, the lies had begun to sound far more damaging and dramatic. For instance, Eleesha had told Ellery about an instance when his sister had been extremely rude to her. While he had always believed in the importance of supporting his wife against verbal abuse, he didn't know what to think about Eleesha's accusation due to her tendency toward lying. Ellery feels like it is difficult to decipher his wife's sincerity. He fears that her habits may have darker implications for her personality. Ellery finds it difficult to be emotionally intimate with Eleesha because he feels like she is undeserving of his honesty when she constantly disrespects him with her lies.

How Deception Warps Relationship Dynamics

Perhaps the most damaging consequence of deception is the shift it creates in your relationship's foundation. Every lie sets off a chain reaction:

- The deceived partner starts to second guess everything.
- The liar becomes defensive, secretive, and often resentful.
- Real connection is replaced with role play and suspicion.

Over time, a relationship rooted in dishonesty becomes a performance. Even when you want to show up authentically, you can't be sure how to begin.

Repeated deception also creates a lopsided power dynamic. The person who holds the truth, holds the power. And that imbalance makes real intimacy impossible.

As painful as it is, confronting this reality is necessary. You can't heal what you don't name. If you want to rebuild trust, you have to be willing to dismantle the structures that deception created.

Rebuilding Trust, One Honest Act at a Time

Here's the truth: you can't rebuild trust overnight. If you've been caught in a pattern of deception, your partner's suspicion and anger are a natural response. Even if they want to forgive you, part of them will be bracing for disappointment.

Rebuilding trust requires patience, humility, and a sustained commitment to transparency. You must be prepared for the process to take longer than you want it to, and to feel more painful than you expect.

Here are steps you can take to begin repairing the damage:

- **Own your actions completely.** Avoid minimizing, deflecting, or blaming. Just say, "This is what I did." "This is why I did it."
- **Offer a genuine apology.** Not the "I'm sorry you feel that way" variety. Apologize for the impact, not just the intention.
- **Invite your partner's perspective.** Let them express how your deception hurt them. Listen without interrupting or defending yourself.
- **Ask what they need to feel safe again.** Be prepared that their requests may feel inconvenient or humbling. This is part of earning

trust back.
- **Demonstrate change with your actions.** Whether it's cutting off contact with someone, sharing passwords, or attending counseling, you must prove that you're serious.
- **Reflect on the root cause.** Why did you feel the need to lie? What insecurities or fears drove you? Until you answer this, the pattern will return (Davis, 2023).

Remember: *Even if your partner chooses not to continue the relationship, you can still grow. The work you do now can prevent the same wounds from repeating in the future.*

Moving Forward, With Courage and Compassion

If you're reading this chapter because you've deceived someone you love, you might feel a mix of shame, regret, and longing. That's normal. You're not alone in your mistakes, and you are not beyond redemption.

Healing from deception is one of the hardest journeys any relationship can face. It requires both partners to be vulnerable in ways that may feel terrifying. It demands the courage to face your shadows and the humility to accept accountability without excuses.

But if you are willing to do this work, consistently and sincerely, trust can be rebuilt. Maybe not exactly as it was, but in a form that is deeper and more honest than before.

Remember: the truth you're avoiding is never as destructive as the lie you tell to cover it. In the end, honesty, however uncomfortable, is always the most loving choice.

In the next chapter, we'll explore **Degradation of the Person You Love**, and how belittling those closest to you slowly unravels the bonds of respect and affection that sustain healthy connection.

XI

- Elisabeth Kubler-Ross

"The moment you degrade others, you degrade yourself."

10

Degradation of the Person You Love

When the Jokes Stop Feeling Funny

I magine this: you're sitting with your partner at a dinner table surrounded by friends. The evening is warm, full of chatter and shared stories. You lean into each other's familiar rhythms, the ones that feel safe and effortless, until your partner opens their mouth and says something that leaves you cold.

A story you once confided in them, a moment you shared when your self worth was at its lowest, is suddenly on display for everyone's entertainment. You try to laugh along, your face tight, your stomach sinking. In that instant, it feels like everyone is in on the joke but you.

Later, you'll replay this scene in your mind. You'll wonder if you overreacted. You'll wonder why the person who's supposed to protect you chose, instead, to showcase your vulnerability like a party trick.

This is what degradation looks like. Not always explosive. Sometimes it creeps in disguised as humor, disguised as just being honest, disguised as love. And it chips away at the trust you thought you had.

Introduction to Degradation

The word degradation carries weight. It means to reduce someone to something less than they are, to humiliate, to diminish, to strip away a sense of dignity (Williams, 2023).

In some contexts, like consensual sexual role play, it can be neutral or even positive. But in everyday relationships, degradation is rarely benign. It's a choice to make the other person small, and it often signals an underlying desire to control or to elevate oneself at the other's expense.

Healthy relationships are built on the idea that your partner is your equal. You might not always agree. You might not always see eye to eye. But at the core, you respect each other. When degradation takes hold, that respect begins to erode.

And when the dynamic shifts from partnership to superiority and subordination, the harm can be deep. **Repeated degradation doesn't just injure someone's feelings, it rewrites their sense of worth.** The person you love may begin to wonder if they deserve that treatment. Over time, they can come to believe the ugly things you say.

In romantic relationships, the stakes are especially high because of the vulnerability that closeness requires. You share secrets, fears, insecurities, trusting they'll be met with tenderness. But when that trust is met with ridicule, the betrayal cuts deep.

Forms of Degradation

Degradation doesn't always look like yelling or name calling. It isn't confined to bruising arguments or public humiliation, though it often escalates there. More often, it starts quietly. A dismissive comment. A backhanded compliment. A refusal to acknowledge your needs.

The common thread is that degradation uses your vulnerability as ammunition. The things you've shared in trust are turned into tools to keep you in your place.

Here are some of the ways degradation can show up:

- **Humiliation in public:** Making a private struggle into a spectacle to win laughs or sympathy from others.
- **Belittling language:** Dismissing your thoughts as stupid, trivial, or childish.
- **Controlling behavior:** Insisting you do tasks that serve no purpose but to demonstrate their power over you.
- **Gaslighting:** Rewriting reality so you question your perception and memory. For example, telling you that you're paranoid when you catch them flirting with someone else.
- **Attacks on identity:** Mocking your appearance, your intelligence, your family, or your faith.
- **Invasive "teasing":** Sharing secrets or insecurities you've entrusted to them.
- **Dismissal of emotions:** Refusing to acknowledge your hurt or accusing you of being "too sensitive."

Even when the tone is casual or framed as a joke, the message is clear: you're lesser. And the more often you hear it, the more likely you are to believe it. (Duvaux, 2022)

The Impact on the Victim

Humiliation is a form of psychological violence. And like all violence, it is designed to establish dominance. One person exerts power by tearing the other down.

When you're the target of degradation, you have only a handful of ways to respond, and none of them heal the wound. You might try to laugh it off, swallow your discomfort, and pretend it didn't matter. Or you might react in anger, which often only deepens the conflict. Either way, the damage lingers.

Over time, repeated degradation can lead to:

- **Anxiety and hypervigilance:** You're always bracing for the next blow.
- **Erosion of self esteem:** You start to internalize the contempt.
- **Social withdrawal:** You avoid shared spaces for fear of embarrassment.
- **Trust issues:** You struggle to believe anyone's kindness is genuine.
- **Depression and hopelessness:** You feel stuck, unseen, and unworthy of love.
- **Trauma responses:** In severe cases, prolonged humiliation can contribute to post traumatic stress and suicidal thoughts (Enright, 2018; Anvar Sadath et al., 2024).

It's important to name this for what it is: abuse. It doesn't matter if you believe you "deserve it." It doesn't matter if your partner insists they're "only joking." You deserve respect. Full stop.

Examples and Real Life Scenarios

Aerielle has worked as an accountant in her husband's firm for most of her career. She is a diligent worker. She never turns in any of her work late. She is friendly and cooperative with her colleagues. Her work is always organized. Despite all her efforts and 10 years of service, Aerielle was never given a salary increment. Newer colleagues joined their firm later than Aerielle and have enjoyed both increments and promotions. It embarrasses Aerielle to think about how everyone knows her husband devalues her efforts. In the presence of others, he likes to make off hand comments about how Aerielle "owes" him for her career. She thinks about her husband, who cannot care enough about her feelings to be respectful and feels a deep hatred towards herself for not speaking up against him. As an introverted, non confrontational person, Aerielle responds to the pain of her indignity with silence. Years of bottling in stress and embarrassment causes Aerielle to suffer from post traumatic stress. Even after their eventual divorce, it takes several years of therapy for Aerielle to feel she is worthy of love and respect.

Chris and Jessica have been in a relationship for two years. They share an apartment, which they pitch in to pay rent and manage other expenses. Jessica's job as a lawyer and five years of seniority over Chris, who just graduated from college a year ago, accounts for her earning a higher income than her boyfriend. While the couple loves each other deeply, Jessica always makes a point of holding her formidable income over Chris. Hearing his girlfriend gloat about how much money she can make and contribute to the relationship makes Chris feel insecure and terrible about his abilities. Especially in the instances where Jessica uses the subject as an opportunity to poke fun at Chris. He feels like he is constantly being disrespected in his relationship. Everything only seems to get worse when they are with friends. Jessica uses her audience as a way of powering her ego. She makes quips at Chris's expense, enjoying the way his embarrassment allowed her to become the life of the party. Over time, Chris develops terrible social anxiety and avoids gatherings with friends altogether. He avoids speaking up at work and withdraws into himself, constantly fearing instances where others would betray and humiliate him. Even after the eventual end of the relationship, Chris still has trouble trusting others.

Why We Degrade the People We Love

If you're the person doing the degrading, you may feel uncomfortable admitting it. You might hear the word abuse and think, *That's too strong.*

But it's essential to understand that degrading someone doesn't always come from malice.

Sometimes it comes from:

- **Unresolved shame:** You can't tolerate your own feelings of inadequacy, so you project them.
- **Childhood conditioning:** If you were degraded by parents or caregivers, you may have learned to equate belittling with power.
- **Insecurity:** You're afraid of being insignificant, so you keep your partner beneath you.
- **Control:** You feel safest when you hold the upper hand.
- **Resentment:** You haven't learned how to express hurt or disappointment constructively.

None of this excuses the behavior. But it does help explain why it happens. And when you understand your patterns, you have a chance to change them.

Addressing Degradation

If you've realized you have a pattern of degrading your partner, you might feel guilt or shame. It's tempting to deflect, to insist it isn't that serious. But real healing requires owning the harm you've caused.

Start by asking yourself some hard questions:

- What do I gain by humiliating this person?
- Do I feel more powerful when I make them feel small?
- When did I first learn that belittling was acceptable?
- What am I afraid would happen if I treated my partner with respect and compassion?

Coaching can be a powerful space to explore these questions without judgment. If you want to keep your relationship, you'll need to commit to doing this work. Because no apology, no single gesture, can undo years of contempt.

Rebuilding Respect

Once degradation has entered a relationship, rebuilding respect is delicate work. The person you love has learned to expect your scorn. Even if they still care for you, they may not feel safe trusting you again. This is where consistency matters more than promises.

Here are some steps you can take:

- **Own your actions.** Name the behavior for what it is. Don't minimize, don't rationalize.
- **Offer a sincere apology.** One that acknowledges the impact, not just the intention.
- **Ask what your partner needs.** Some will need time apart. Others will need reassurance. Some may want to set new boundaries.
- **Respect their process.** Healing from degradation takes time. You don't get to dictate how quickly they forgive you.
- **Practice transparency.** Share your feelings and fears. Let them see your willingness to be vulnerable.
- **Invest in self awareness.** Learn to recognize your triggers before

they become cruelty.
- **Commit to growth.** Whether through coaching or honest reflection, keep showing up for the work. (Smith, 2021)

Moving Forward, Together or Apart

Not every relationship survives the aftermath of chronic degradation. Sometimes the harm has gone too far. Sometimes the most loving choice is to part ways so you can each heal.

But if you and your partner choose to rebuild, know that it can be done. It requires courage, yours and theirs. It requires humility and patience. And it requires the understanding that love alone isn't enough.

Love must be paired with respect, safety, and empathy. Without these, no amount of affection can keep you whole.

If you take only one thing from this chapter, let it be this: how you treat the person you love matters more than anything else. Every word, every action either builds trust or chips away at it.

The next chapter will explore **Depreciation of Your Partner's Self Esteem**, and how slowly undermining someone's confidence is one of the most corrosive patterns a relationship can endure.

XII

-Eleanor Roosevelt

"We are afraid to care too much, for fear that the other person does not care at all."

11

Depreciation of Your Partner's Self-Esteem

I Am Too Big to Be Belittled, I Think?

Have you ever had your heart sink because of a single careless remark from the person you trusted most? Maybe you were joking around, sharing something vulnerable, and your partner brushed it off with an eye roll or a sigh. Maybe you tried to open up about something that mattered to you, your body, your career, your dreams, and were met with teasing or an awkward silence.

And even though you told yourself it's not that big a deal, a part of you shrank inside. You swallowed the hurt. You smiled to keep the peace. But deep down, a seed of doubt took root: Maybe I really am too sensitive. *Maybe I don't deserve better.*

This is how self esteem depreciation begins. Not always in obvious explosions of cruelty, but in the slow drip of dismissiveness, sarcasm, or indifference. Over time, these micro moments can corrode the foundation of love itself, until you no longer recognize the confident, hopeful person you were when the relationship began.

As a coach, I've seen how easily we can become blind to this erosion, especially when the behavior is so subtle, so normalized, that it hardly feels worth mentioning. But trust me when I say this: **the small things matter**. If you care about the person you love, and about the relationship you're building, it's worth learning how to protect and nurture their sense of self.

Introduction to Self Esteem Depreciation

Think of your relationship as a bridge stretched between two solid cliffs. That bridge is trust, mutual respect, and belief in each other's goodness. Now imagine one of those cliffs beginning to crumble, just a little at a time. A stone loosened here. A crack spreading there. No loud collapse, just a slow erosion that weakens everything holding you up.

This is what happens when your words, actions, or even your tone begin to chip away at your partner's self esteem. When their confidence feels fragile, the entire bridge starts to tilt. You can still cross it, but it takes more effort. You second guess your footing. You hold your breath and wonder if this time, it might finally give way.

Self esteem isn't an accessory that your partner can simply take off and hang up at the door. It's the lens through which they see their worth, and the lens through which they experience your love. When that lens is scratched or clouded, it distorts everything.

You may think, I'm just teasing, they know I love them. But love is not always enough to counterbalance repeated messages, spoken or unspoken, that they're not measuring up. And the longer this goes unacknowledged, the harder it becomes to undo.

Impact on the Victim

Living in a relationship that steadily drains your self esteem can feel a lot like living with an unpredictable bully. One minute, everything seems fine. The next, your partner makes a comment that lands like a slap you can't see coming.

I've worked with countless clients who say they'd rather have been yelled at outright than subjected to this low grade, chronic undermining. Because when someone insults you, you know it's an attack. But when someone depreciates you with a shrug or a smirk, you start to question your own reality. Am I overreacting? Am I too sensitive?

This confusion is part of why depreciation is so damaging. It forces the victim to internalize the blame. Over time, their inner voice grows harsh and critical, echoing the words they've heard from their partner. You're not good enough. You're overthinking it. You should be grateful anyone puts up with you.

The psychological fallout can be immense:

- Chronic anxiety, as the person braces for the next dismissal or judgment.
- Hyper vigilance, constantly scanning for signs of disapproval.
- Loss of trust, both in the relationship and in their own instincts.
- A gnawing shame that whispers, "You deserve this."
- Depression and a sense of helplessness.
- Physical symptoms, headaches, insomnia, fatigue, as their body absorbs the stress.

Studies confirm the health impacts are real. According to Banks (2024), prolonged stress in intimate relationships is linked to suppressed immune function, increased inflammation, and higher risk of chronic illness.

If this sounds familiar, please know: You are not imagining it. You are not weak. And you are not alone.

Examples and Scenarios

Alicea and Darrell have been married for five years. At thirty, Alicea is eager to become a mother because of her biological clock. However, whenever the topic of child rearing comes forth in conversation, Darrell tends to change the subject or go silent. While Alicea understands that her husband can be nervous about introducing such a significant change into their life, she is eager to discuss the subject. Darrell is usually strong willed about his opinions and beliefs. Whenever he does not agree with something, he expresses his disapproval outright. He finds it hard to hold back his tongue, even when he knows it can hurt others. He expresses his emotions in jabs and jokes at the other person's character. The issue is that Darrell is not very simple or subtle about communicating his emotions. For instance, he jokingly tells Alicea that he will break up with her if she ever gets pregnant "on his watch." Other lines of his poor brain to mouth filter have repeatedly made Alicea feel terrible about herself. Darrell's need to control conversations and insulting language make Alicea feel bad about herself. Alicea feels too unconfident to speak up for herself. Oblivious to Alicea's feelings, Darrell continues to carry on with his behavior. Alicea's poor self esteem makes her feel distant and unattached to him. The lack of intimacy and emotional understanding that results, leave them both unsatisfied with the relationship.

Jaime and Will have been together for four years. They both love each other and have lived together for two years. Yet, the two share very different perspectives on how they can best express their emotions. Jaime is outgoing and has many friends with whom she constantly interacts at social events. Will is more introverted than his girlfriend. From the early stage of their relationship, the dynamic between them had been for Will to rely on Jaime *as his guide to social situations. However, years of leaning on Jaime as his compass had caused the dependency to feel forced and oppressive. Jaime's actions to "help" Will seemed patronizing and, at times, hurtful. Will does not like how Jaime tries to coordinate his outfits. He also does not appreciate the comments she makes about how he could improve his career. Telling Jaime what she does wrong only erupts in friction and fighting, which they both detest. With time, Will feels sick of himself because of the stance he has to take in his relationship. Wearing clothes that feel too planned out to be casual and constantly listening to his girlfriend go on about how he could improve himself makes Will feel like his identity has little value. Will begins to resent Jaime for how she makes him feel about himself. The resentment causes tension between them.*

Preventing Self Esteem Depreciation

If you've realized that your words or actions might have contributed to your partner's self doubt, take a moment to breathe. You are not condemned by your mistakes. You are simply human, like the rest of us, sometimes clumsy, sometimes careless, but capable of learning a different way.

The good news is that you can start repairing this dynamic right now. Many of the habits that depreciate self esteem are subtle and unintentional. With awareness and intention, they can be replaced with healthier patterns.

Here are some ways to begin:

- **Mind your body language.** Sometimes, the damage isn't in what you say but in how you say it, or don't say it. An eye roll when they share an idea. A sigh when they tell a story. These small gestures accumulate. Try to stay present. Look them in the eye. Show them

that you're listening, even if you disagree.
- **Don't offer unsolicited advice.** Especially when your partner is sharing something vulnerable. When you jump in to fix, you can accidentally send the message that they're incompetent or incapable. Instead, ask: Do you want my perspective or just my support?
- **Stay engaged.** One of the most powerful gifts you can give is your attention. Not distracted half listening while you check your phone, but real presence. It says: I care about your experience. You matter to me.
- **Respect their autonomy.** If your love feels like control, if you're always telling them what to do or how to do it, they will start to feel smaller, not safer. Supporting someone means helping them build their own confidence, not making them dependent on yours.
- **Watch your humor.** Humor is wonderful, unless it comes at your partner's expense. Teasing that cuts too close to the bone can leave lasting scars. If they look hurt, pause. Check in. Apologize if needed.

These practices don't mean you'll never slip up. You will. What matters is that you're willing to notice when you do, and to repair the moment with honesty and care.

Supporting and Rebuilding Self Esteem

If you've contributed to your partner's self doubt, it can be tempting to avoid talking about it altogether. But silence is its own kind of wound. Naming what happened is the first step to healing.

Here are some ways to begin that conversation and lay a foundation for repair:

- **Identify the patterns.** Together, look at what kinds of comments or

behaviors have been most hurtful. Be specific. When you called me lazy in front of your friends, it felt humiliating.
- **Take ownership.** This is not the time for justifications. "No. I was only joking." "No, You're too sensitive." Just acknowledgment: "I see how much this hurt you, I'm sorry."
- **Offer reassurance.** Let them know you value them. Speak to their strengths. You're kind, you're resilient, you matter to me, and mean it.
- **Encourage self compassion.** If your partner starts to spiral into self blame or self criticism, gently remind them: Your worth isn't defined by any single moment. You are more than this.
- **Create rituals of affirmation.** This might mean leaving them a note before work, or naming one thing you admire about them each day. Small gestures rebuild safety.
- **Invite professional support.** Therapy can help your partner process old wounds and learn to trust their own worth again. It can also help you both navigate the complex layers of guilt, grief, and hope that often come with relationship repair.

Remember: healing isn't linear. There will be days when your partner struggles to believe you. When they flinch at a word or withdraw into old patterns. That doesn't mean you're failing. It just means their nervous system is still learning it's safe again. Stay steady. Be patient. Offer grace to them, and to yourself.

Moving Forward Together

If there's one truth I wish every couple could hold close, it's this:
Loving someone means you become part of their story of themselves.
Every time you speak, every time you look at them, you're either reinforcing the belief that they are worthy of respect and love, or you're

chipping away at it.

None of us will get this perfectly. But all of us can commit to trying, to becoming more aware, more intentional, more compassionate.

Because in the end, your relationship isn't defined by how many times you hurt each other, it's defined by how many times you chose to try again, to do better, to love each other more skillfully.

As you move forward, I invite you to keep this question close: What would it feel like to be someone whose presence builds others up instead of wearing them down?

I now invite you to read the Conclusion of Removing The "D" From Anger

XIII

-T.S. Elliot

"Every moment is a fresh beginning."

12

Conclusion

Acknowledging our faults is never easy, especially when they exist within the vulnerable framework of our closest relationships. By choosing to read this book, by leaning into discomfort and exploring strategies that confront societal shame, personal guilt, and the psychological weight of destructive habits, you've placed yourself on a path that many avoid. And that choice, however difficult, is courageous.

The hardest part of real change is the bravery it takes to face what's broken. But if you're reading this, it means you've already taken that crucial first step: *recognizing the need for healing and seeking the tools to grow.* That, in itself, is an act of strength, one that deserves to be honored.

Relationships rarely exist in the simplicity of black and white. They're layered with nuance, shaped by history, emotion, and perspective. But when we grant ourselves the self awareness to approach them with mindfulness and intention, we begin to cultivate the kind of connection that not only transforms our relationships but also our lives.

Take a moment to consider how far you've come from when you first began reading this book. Has your perspective on destructive relationship habits changed? Do you understand the emotions, thoughts, and beliefs that cause you to behave in certain ways? Most importantly, do you want to change the course that your relationships may have taken? As I observe with most of my clients, the shame of being the "wrong" one in a relationship can sometimes cripple even the most beautiful connections. If you truly love someone, you deserve to experience the joy and fulfillment that comes from honoring who they are by caring for them in ways that respect their boundaries and individuality. As you reflect on your journey of confronting destructive habits and the consequences they carry, take a moment to recognize how far you've come, from someone who may have once lacked this level of awareness to someone who is now capable of seeing things with greater clarity and objectivity. You have all the knowledge you need to change your life; all that is left is for you to have the courage to move forward.

It takes continual practice, revisitation, and consistency for the change we need to uproot negative behaviors within our lives. As you learned in this book, a challenging part about reconciling your mistakes with the strategies needed to overcome them is having the time and patience to deal with how overwhelming this can all be for your partner. Remember, your partner has faced the brunt of the detrimental effects that toxic habits can leave on a relationship. They have seen you at your worst and may need time to adjust. While it is certainly painful to witness someone you love struggle to trust the change you genuinely want to implement into your life, this is only a part of the natural process you need to build a healthier connection with them.

In the same way, you may also find it challenging to unlearn some of your toxic habits, even when you are equipped with the knowledge of its legal, financial, and psychological consequences. The truth is that ingrained habits can take time and practice to be swapped for healthier practices. Allow yourself to accept this and have patience with your journey.

CONCLUSION

Writing this book and creating The Ricky C Williams Podcast, based on the core concepts of my professional practice, has been a labor of love. While you can find texts that focus on anger management in the market, it is so much more challenging to find reliable sources of information that deal with more "taboo" elements of destructive anger. I don't believe that any relationship or individual is beyond change. Relationships are far more complex than our abilities to distinguish if they are toxic. I believe that tools like this book can work as guidelines that allow us all to understand how toxic some of our habits tend to be. After all, awareness is one of the primary tools we need to implement long-standing change. As we conclude this book, I am only grateful to you, dear reader, for taking this journey together. We both know that it was hardly pleasant, but one that is instrumental in allowing us all to find the light at the ends of our tunnels.

Epilogue

If you've made it to this point, I want to say something simple but powerful: I'm proud of you.

Not because you've read every chapter, but because you've done something that many people never do: you've faced your anger head on. You've chosen to understand it, not ignore it. You've chosen healing over hiding. And that takes strength. Real strength.

By now, you know that anger is not the enemy. It's a signal, one that tells you something is off, something needs attention, and something must change. When you remove the "D", the destruction from anger, what you're left with is energy, passion, and truth. Those are tools, not threats. And now, you have the power to use them wisely.

This book wasn't written to fix you. You were never broken. It was written to equip you, to give you the tools to take control, to communicate clearly, and to lead with clarity and compassion.

Keep practicing. Keep growing. Keep showing up for yourself and for the people who love you.

And when the anger rises again, as it will, remember: you're not who you used to be. You're stronger. You're more aware. You've done the work. You've removed the "D".

Now walk in that power.

Afterword

Write This On Your Vision Board

"I have now become confident in controlling my anger but also learned how to show empathy to my personal and professional partners. I know how to properly protect my family, which ultimately breaks generational cycles of abuse. It is time for legacy building, focus, and provision."

Continue to listen to The Ricky C Williams Podcast on Spotify and Youtube, as we will continue our journey of healing.

P.S. Thank you so much for reading. If you enjoyed this book, I'd really love it if you could leave a 30 second review and share a photo of you holding the book on Amazon. The QR Code is on the next page. I Love You, **Now G.B.G.....Go Be Great**

REMOVING THE D FROM ANGER BOOK 2025

References

Adamgbo, D. (2023, March 24). Understanding the Difference Between Willful and Malicious Damage to Property. Medium; Medium. https://medium.com/@the_solicitorng/understanding-the-difference-between-willful-and-malicious-damage-to-property-1eb1f4887627

Admin, A. (2019, March 28). Is the Destruction of My Property Domestic Violence? | Domestic Violence Restraining Order Attorneys Morris County NJ | Mt. Olive Domestic Violence Attorneys. Townsend, Tomaio & Newmark. https://www.ttnlaw.com/blog/2019/03/destroying-property-and-restraining-orders/

Allen, L. (2021, October 14). 6 Ways to Know If You're in a Financially Toxic Relationship. Money Done Right. https://moneydoneright.com/personal-finance/building-wealth/financial-abuse/

Anvar Sadath, Katerina Kavalidou, McMahon, E., Malone, K., & McLoughlin, A. (2024). Associations between humiliation, shame, self-harm and suicidality among adolescents and young adults: A systematic review. PLOS ONE, 19(2), e0292691–e0292691. https://doi.org/10.1371/journal.pone.0292691

Australia, H. (2023, March 17). Domestic violence and abusive relationships. Healthdirect. https://www.healthdirect.gov.au/domestic-violence-and-abusive-relationships#:~:text=As%20well%20as%20physical%20injuries%2C%20people%20in%20an

Banks, D. (2024, May 29). 15 Troubling Signs of Emotional Bullying in Relationships. Marriage Advice - Expert Marriage Tips & Advice; Marriage.com. https://www.marriage.com/advice/mental-health/emot

ional-bullying/#:~:text=Emotional%20bullying%20in%20a%20relationship%20is%20a%20form

Beer Becker, D. (2022, March 25). What are the signs of a dysfunctional relationship? Blake Psychology. https://www.blakepsychology.com/2022/03/what-are-the-signs-of-a-dysfunctional-relationship/

Buffalmano, L. (2021). 7 Types of Dysfuntional Relationship (W/Examples). Thepowermoves.com. https://thepowermoves.com/dysfuntional-relationships-dances

Cannon, J. (2021, February 24). 5 Ways Toxic Relationships Change You | Psychology Today. Www.psychologytoday.com. https://www.psychologytoday.com/us/blog/stress-fracture/202102/5-ways-toxic-relationships-change-you

Charlie Health Editorial Team. (2023, April 28). Toxic Relationships & Mental Health | Charlie Health. Www.charliehealth.com. https://www.charliehealth.com/post/how-toxic-relationships-affect-your-mental-health

Cherry, K. (2024, January 31). Emotional Intelligence: How We Perceive, Evaluate, Express, and Control Emotions. Verywell Mind. https://www.verywellmind.com/what-is-emotional-intelligence-2795423

Cohen, E. (2023, May 29). Idealization and Devaluation: What You Need To Know. Charlie Health. https://www.charliehealth.com/post/idealization-and-devaluation-what-you-need-to-know

Cuncic, A. (2021, November 18). Effects of Narcissistic Abuse. Verywell Mind. https://www.verywellmind.com/effects-of-narcissistic-abuse-5208164

Davis, M. (2023, March 5). How to Rebuild Trust in a Marriage After Lying (and Avoid Mistakes). Married Advice. https://marriedadvice.com/how-to-rebuild-trust-in-a-marriage-after-lying/

Davis, T. (2021, April 21). Managing Anger: Tips, Techniques, and Tools | Psychology Today. Www.psychologytoday.com. https://www.ps

ychologytoday.com/us/blog/click-here-happiness/202104/managing-anger-tips-techniques-and-tools

Dr. Bruce Kehr. (2018, January 30). How do I Recover from Trauma and Humiliation? (Part 1). Potomacpsychiatry.com; Potomac Psychiatry .https://www.potomacpsychiatry.com/blog/recover-trauma-humiliation

Drescher, A. (2023, February 22). Narcissistic Love Bombing Cycle: Idealize, Devalue, Discard. Simply Psychology. https://www.simplypsychology.org/narcissistic-love-bombing-cycle.html

Duvaux, A. (2022, July 13). 8 Different Types of Abuse in a Relationship. Marriage Advice - Expert Marriage Tips & Advice. https://www.marriage.com/advice/domestic-violence-and-abuse/types-of-abuse-in-a-relationship/

Dysfunctional Relationships | Saprea. (2023, September 15). Saprea. https://saprea.org/heal/dysfunctional-relationships/

Enright, R. (2018, August 29). How to Overcome the Dangers of Humiliation. Psychology Today. https://www.psychologytoday.com/us/blog/the-forgiving-life/201808/how-overcome-the-dangers-humiliation?msockid=1b797c5ff25c625315c868b7f3dc63fc

Firestone, L. (2011, June 14). Deception and the Destruction of Your Relationship. PsychAlive. https://www.psychalive.org/relationship-infidelity-and-the-real-villain-behind-it/

Fletcher, J., & Sissons, B. (n.d.). Emotional abuse: The short- and long-term effects. Www.medicalnewstoday.com. https://www.medicalnewstoday.com/articles/327080#long-term-effects

Gordon, S. (n.d.). What Are the Signs of Verbal Abuse? Verywell Mind. https://www.verywellmind.com/how-to-recognize-verbal-abuse-bullying-4154087#:~:text=Verbal%20abuse%20is%20a%20type%20of%20emotional%20abuse.

Gupta, S. (n.d.). What to Do If You're in an Unhappy Relationship. Verywell Mind. https://www.verywellmind.com/what-to-do-if-you-re

-in-an-unhappy-relationship-5207633

Guy-Evans, O. (2023, December 7). What Is a Toxic Relationship? 7 Signs and What to Do. Www.simplypsychology.org. https://www.simply psychology.org/toxic-relationships.html

Hammond, C. (2017, March 22). 13 reasons why people abuse. Psych Central. https://psychcentral.com/pro/exhausted-woman/2017/03/13-reasons-why-people-abuse#2

Openr. (2024, January 10).How Social Media Can Destroy Someone's Reputation And Career –Openr.co. https://openr.co/how-social-media-can-destroy-someones-reputation-and-career/

Identifying Cognitive Distortions in Relationships. (2023, December 16). Cognitive Behavioral Therapy Los Angeles. https://cogbtherapy.co m/cbt-blog/cognitive-distortions-in-relationships

JML Law. (2023, February 21). How Defamation Can Negatively Impact Your Life. JML. https://jmllaw.com/how-defamation-can-n egatively-impact-your-life.shtml

Kapoor, A. (2023, June 21). Deception: Major Reason Behind An Unhealthy or Unsuccessful Relationship. Calm Sage - Your Guide to Mental and Emotional Well-Being. https://www.calmsage.com/decepti on-major-reason-behind-an-unhealthy-or-unsuccessful-relationshi p/

Karawadia, F. (2024, August 7). Signs of Appreciation In a Relationship. VeryWell Mindset. https://verywellmindset.com/signs-of-apprec iation-in-a-relationship/#:~:text=Appreciation%3A%201%20Boosts %20self-esteem%20%26%20confidence%20in%20the

Kellot, T. (2023, November 9). How Toxic Relationships Affect Your Mental Health . Science of Mind. https://scienceofmind.org/how-toxic-relationships-affect-your-mental-health/#:~:text=Toxic%20relations hips%20contribute%20significantly%20to%20mental%20health%20i ssues

Marriage.com Editorial Team. (2021, May 17). 15 Signs of a Dysfunc-

REFERENCES

tional Relationship. Marriage Advice - Expert Marriage Tips & Advice. https://www.marriage.com/advice/relationship/signs-of-a-dysfunctional-relationship/

MasterClass. (n.d.). Validation in Relationships: The Importance of Emotional Validation. Master Class. https://www.masterclass.com/articles/validation-in-relationships

Newsome, T. (2016, April 18). 24 Ways You Could Be Hurting Your Partner's Self-Esteem Without Realizing It. Bustle. https://www.bustle.com/articles/155358-24-ways-you-could-be-hurting-your-partners-self-esteem-without-realizing-it

Nollan, J. (2020, August 28). How To Deal With Someone Who Humiliates You In Public. A Conscious Rethink. https://www.aconsciousrethink.com/13950/deal-with-someone-who-humiliates-you-in-public/

Pace, R. (2021, September 27). 20 Signs of Disrespect in a Relationship & How to Deal With It. Marriage Advice - Expert Marriage Tips & Advice. https://www.marriage.com/advice/relationship/signs-of-disrespect-in-a-relationship

Papa Pintor, Y. (2017, August 28). What are the Signs of Dissatisfaction in a Relationship? Step to Health. https://steptohealth.com/signs-dissatisfaction-relationship/

PsychAlive. (2013, August 22). Toxic Relationships: Is Your Relationship Toxic? PsychAlive. https://www.psychalive.org/toxic-relationship/

Raqeeb, F. (2024, May 23). Defamation: What to Do if Someone Is Trying to Damage Your Reputation. RFB Legal. https://rfblegal.co.uk/insights/defamation-what-to-do-if-someone-is-trying-to-damage-your-reputation/

Rose Emery, L., & Swanson, H. (2024, February 20). How To Rebuild Trust After A Betrayal. Bustle. https://www.bustle.com/wellness/how-to-gain-you-partners-trust-back

Sameer Somal. (2022, October 12). Online Reputation Management Firm. Blog | Tech Educators | Blue Ocean Global Technology. https://www.blueoceanglobaltech.com/blog/emotional-distress-damages/

Shafir, H. (2022, March 1). Signs of Emotional Neglect In Adulthood. Choosing Therapy. https://www.choosingtherapy.com/emotional-neglect-in-adults/

Smith, L. (2021, February). 8 Ways To Build Trust In A Relationship (+ 8 Trust Exercises). A Conscious Rethink. https://www.aconsciousrethink.com/15249/how-to-build-trust-in-a-relationship/

Sterbenz, C., & Davis, D.-M. (2020, June 16). 12 common phrases and terms that are actually racist or offensive. Business Insider; Insider. https://www.businessinsider.com/offensive-phrases-that-people-still-use-2013-11#8-eskimo-8 6 signs of a toxic relationship (and how to end them). (n.d.). Calm Blog. https://www.calm.com/blog/toxic-relationships

Stritof, S. (n.d.). How to Tell If Your Spouse Is Lying. Verywell Mind. https://www.verywellmind.com/how-to-tell-if-spouse-is-lying-2300996

Tonkin, M., & Burell, A. (2014). Psychological impacts - Property Crime: Criminological and Psychological Perspectives. Ebrary. https://ebrary.net/266964/psychology/psychological_impacts#172782

Townsend, Tomaio & Newmark, LLC. (2019, March 28). Is the Destruction of My Property Domestic Violence? | Domestic Violence Restraining Order Attorneys Morris County NJ | Mt. Olive Domestic Violence Attorneys. Townsend, Tomaio & Newmark. https://www.ttnlaw.com/blog/2019/03/destroying-property-and-restraining-orders/

Wakefield, M. (2023, July 15). The Cycle of Narcissistic Abuse. Narcissistic Abuse Rehab. https://www.narcissisticabuserehab.com/cycle-of-narcissistic-abuse/#:~:text=The%20victim%20is%20subjected%20to%20a%20continuous%20stream

Williams, H. (2023, February 21). What Does Degrade Mean In A

Relationship. RelationRise. https://relationrise.com/what-does-degra
de-mean-in-a-relationship/

About the Author

Ricky C. Williams is a nationally recognized anger management coach, certified mediator, and advocate for emotional well-being. Born and raised in Lake Charles, Louisiana, Ricky earned his Bachelor of Science in Business Marketing from Grambling State University before dedicating his career to helping individuals transform their lives.

With over a decade of experience guiding men and professionals to master their emotions, Ricky has become known for blending evidence-based techniques with real-world wisdom. As a dynamic keynote speaker and trainer, he inspires audiences at conferences, corporate events, and educational seminars to adopt practical strategies for better relationships, healthier communication, and lasting self-control.

Ricky also hosts **The Ricky C Williams Podcast,** where he shares insights on emotional resilience and conflict resolution. When he's not writing, speaking, or coaching, he enjoys spending time with his children, exploring new hobbies, and passionately supporting the Texas Rangers.

You can connect with me on:

- https://www.therickycwilliamspodcast.com
- https://x.com/1rickycwilliams
- https://www.facebook.com/1rickycwilliams
- https://www.youtube.com/@TheRickyCWilliamsPodcast
- https://www.instagram.com/rickycwilliams

www.ingramcontent.com/pod-product-compliance
Lightning Source LLC
Chambersburg PA
CBHW060526090426
42735CB00011B/2384